Fitness for Full-Contact Fighters

Christoph Delp

Fitness for Full-Contact Fighters

Training for Muay Thai, Kick-Boxing, Karate, and Taekwondo

BLUE SNAKE BOOKS
Berkeley, California

Published by Blue Snake Books/Frog, Ltd.

Blue Snake Books/Frog, Ltd. books are distributed by
North Atlantic Books
P.O. Box 12327
Berkeley, California 94712

Cover photograph by Erwin Wenzel
Cover and book design by Brad Greene
Edited by Adrienne Armstrong
Printed in Singapore
Distributed to the book trade by Publishers Group West

Blue Snake Books' publications are available through most bookstores. For further information, call 800-337-2665 or visit our websites at www.northatlanticbooks.com or www.bluesnakebooks.com.

Substantial discounts on bulk quantities are available to corporations, professional associations, and other organizations. For details and discount information, contact our special sales department.

PLEASE NOTE: The author, the creators, and the publishers of this book disclaim any liabilities for loss in connection with following any of the practices, exercises, and advice contained herein. To reduce the chance of injury or any other harm, the reader should consult a professional before undertaking this or any other martial arts, movement, meditative arts, health, or exercise program. The instructions and advice printed in this book are not in any way intended as a substitute for medical care or mental or emotional counseling with a licensed physician or healthcare provider.

Library of Congress Cataloging-in-Publication Data

Delp, Christoph, 1974-
    [Fitness für Kampfsportler. English]
    Fitness for full-contact fighters : training for muay thai, kick-boxing, karate, and taekwondo / by Christoph Delp.
        p. cm.
    Summary: "An indispensable fitness training guide for all martial artists helping them to optimise their ability to perform through the development of flexibility, stamina, and power"—Provided by publisher.
    Includes bibliographical references.
    ISBN-13: 978-1-58394-157-7 (trade paper)
    ISBN-10: 1-58394-157-6 (trade paper)
    1. Martial arts—Training. I. Title.
    GV1102.7.T7D45 2006
    613.7'148—dc22

                                    2006010163
                                    CIP

1 2 3 4 5 6 7 8 9 TWP 12 11 10 09 08 07 06

Expression of Thanks by the Author

I thank my family for their support, Oliver Glatow for his help in the photo production, Eckhard Glatow for his support, the photographer Nopphadol Viwatkamolwat for the nice pictures, and, of course, the martial artists Tui, Vanessa, Christian, Ernst, Giovanni, and Steffen for their excellent cooperation.

✖ Martin Albers (World and European Kick-Boxing Champion)

Contents

Part I: Basics

CHAPTER 1

Basics of Fitness Training

Do you want to dominate your opponent with explosive kicks and a hard series of punches? Do you want to be fit and fully focused up to the last round and excite spectators with your style? Do you want to regain your fitness level quickly after strenuous training sessions? These are the goals of many fighters in the areas of Muay Thai, kick-boxing, karate, and taekwondo.

You will achieve these goals by adding fitness sessions—for flexibility, stamina, and power—to your martial arts training in combination with the correct nutrition. The *flexibility training* will enable you to perform technically correct high-kicking techniques. The *stamina training* will provide the staying power for extended time periods. The *power training* gets your muscles in shape for the powerful execution of techniques and to withstand the opponent's attacks. If you also include an appropriate diet, excess weight will soon disappear and you can start competing in your optimum weight class.

This book provides martial arts athletes with the fundamentals of fitness training and correct nutrition. The fitness components of flexibility, stamina, and power are described in detail with suggestions on how to improve your performance level in these areas. Training plans show the sensible combination of martial arts and fitness training. Use the fitness training to reach your targets in martial arts at the earliest possible stage.

The Book's Structure

Part I provides the basics of fitness training, as well as advice on correct nutrition for martial arts athletes.

Part II is dedicated to stretching. You will learn the most important methods and rules before the exercises are described.

Part III describes the stamina training. You will learn which intensity and which types of sport are best suited for the training.

Part IV contains useful information about power training. You will also be introduced to the best methods and exercises.

Part V describes the basics required for training plans. Furthermore, programs are introduced that effectively combine martial arts and fitness training. In this way, you will soon be able to improve your performance potential in martial arts.

What Is Fitness?

Fitness for the martial arts athlete means a good physical condition and the ability to perform. You are in a position to call on your current best possible performance potential. Your techniques are at a high level and you are fully fit in the areas of stamina and power. In such physical shape you can successfully compete in fights.

Building up or maintaining your fitness requires regular training sessions for your body as a stimulus; otherwise, the performance level of your body will deteriorate rather than improve.

The primary components of physical fitness are stamina, power, flexibility, coordination, and speed. To improve your martial arts performance by fitness training, as is the aim of this book, you must particularly concentrate on training sessions for stamina, power, and flexibility. In addition, special exercises aimed at the improvement of coordination and speed can also be carried out.

Flexibility

Flexibility training enables the optimal execution of all fight techniques, especially high-kicking techniques. You also reduce the risk of injury when you stretch tight muscles prior to training.

Power

Muscle power must be developed through training to increase the level of physical performance. Regular training significantly increases the power of your punches and kicks. In addition, the training can be aimed at correcting the imbalance of certain muscles, which can be caused by injuries or by the repetition of one-sided activities.

Stamina

Stamina training improves both physical and mental performance. The training forms part of the martial arts exercises—for example, when working out on the punching bag or pads, and in sparring. Carry out extra stamina training sessions to lower the pulse rate when resting or under physical strain. This will provide extra fitness and concentration in competition. It also helps in mastering stressful situations and in preventing cardiovascular disorders.

Coordination

Coordination is already integrated into the sport-specific training—for example, in difficult combinations of techniques. The fitness program can be extended by means of specific exercises, such as the one-leg stand (see pp. 198–199). In this way you improve your balance and reflexes, which is of particular importance after an injury.

Speed

Recreational sports do not require as much attention to speed training as to the aforementioned fitness components. However, on a competitive level, speed is decisive. To this end, it must be included in the sport-specific training. In addition, advanced athletes can improve their speed in power training by carrying out some exercises in accordance with the resilience method (takeoff power) (see p. 114). Moreover, speed can be increased by sprinting for 55 or 65 yards.

Training Stimulus—The Principle of Super Compensation

In fitness training the body is stimulated to develop a greater performance potential. This requires balanced training of all the body's muscle groups.

Higher-Level Training Stimulus

Your body reacts to physical strain with adaptation processes. If an above-level stimulus is part of the training—that is, increased performance over that of the previous training session is called for—the organ-

ism will produce a greater performance level after a phase of regeneration. This process, which leads to an improved starting level, is called super compensation. However, the better your body has been trained, the more minimal your performance improvements will be. If, instead, the body receives only minor stimuli, and is not challenged to perform, there will be no adaptation but, at best, the performance level will be maintained. Without stimulation the body's performance will decrease. If, for example, a fractured leg requires a cast, the muscles of the protected leg clearly shrink within days. The intensity and training method confronting the body are of decisive importance to the adaptation process and performance improvement. In stamina training, for example, it is possible to increase the distance continually, and in power training heavier weights can be used. Martial arts training addresses all fitness components. In the process, those areas of the body will improve that have been subjected to an above-level training stimulus.

Regeneration Phase

The organism needs a regeneration phase after the training stimulus. It is in this phase that the body adapts itself to the new stimulus. The starting level improves as a consequence of the above-level training stimulus. The time required for regeneration and adaptation depends on the intensity of the stimulation, the training condition, and the training method used. For example, following a power training session using the stamina power method, the muscles used in training require less regeneration time than required after an intensive training session with the muscle development method (see pp. 112–113). The time needed for regeneration can be cut by a reasonable program—for example, easy jogging and ample sleep.

Optimum Training Effect

An optimum effect of the training will be achieved if the break between two training sessions has been scheduled properly. When the body does not receive sufficient time for regeneration, the result is excessive strain, which will have a negative impact on the performance level. If, however, the break between two training sessions is too long, the body's performance level will go down and performance improvement is no longer feasible. Due to the number of components affecting the length of the regeneration phase, it is impossible to arrive at an exact length of time. Athletes should strive to increasingly understand their body, so that they can plan for optimum training. A guideline for beginners is to rest for a period of one to three days between two similar training sessions, depending on how intensively they carried out the first session. If ambitious athletes wish to engage in fitness training frequently, they should switch between different methods. They could, for example, carry out one sport-specific session one day and do stamina training the next.

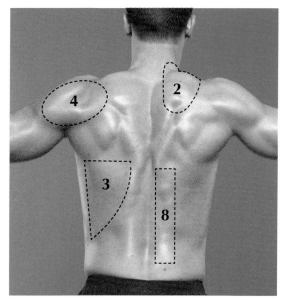

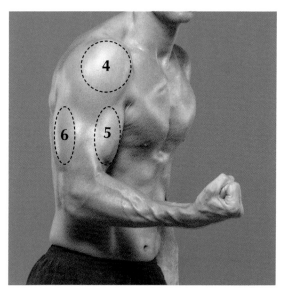

CHAPTER 2

The Muscle Groups

Here you will learn about the most important muscle groups for your fitness training.

1. The Chest Muscles

The pectoral muscles cover the chest and define its shape. They participate in nearly all the movements of the shoulder joint. Their primary function is to push the arm forward. The antagonist to the chest muscles is the back muscles, as it is their main function to pull the arm backward. Strengthening of the chest muscles results in greater punching power.

Stretching exercises: D 3, D 4
Strengthening exercises: K 1, K 2, K 3, K 4, K 5

2. The Neck Muscles

The muscle cords of the trapezius run across the shoulders and the upper part of the back up to the neck. The primary functions of the neck muscles are to keep the head straight and to lift, lower, or pull back the shoulders, depending on which part of the trapezius muscles is used. The strengthening of these muscles improves the ability to withstand punishment, as hits to the head can be absorbed better.

Stretching exercises: D 1, D 2
Strengthening exercises: K 8, K 9, K 10

3. The Upper Back Muscles

The broad back muscles shape the back. As a marked feature they define the frequently desired V-shape. Their primary function is to pull the arm backward (antagonist to the chest muscles), or downward from a raised position. The training of these muscles enables powerful clinching of the opponent in an infight. These muscles must be strengthened in conjunction with the chest muscles; otherwise, the result will be an imbalance of the muscle groups, which increases susceptibility to injuries.

Stretching exercises: D 9, D 10, D 11
Strengthening exercises: K 11, K 12, K 13, K 14

4. The Shoulder Muscles

This muscle group is also known as the deltoid muscle. It covers the shoulder joint and forms the round shape of the shoulder. The deltoid muscle can be differentiated into three areas: the front part has the primary function of pushing the arm forward, the lateral part spreads the arm away from the body, and the rear part pulls the arm backward. Training of the shoulder muscles develops greater punching and pushing power in fist and elbow techniques. In addition, the training, particularly of the lateral and rear parts, prevents disproportionate muscle development due to one-sided exercises.

Stretching exercises: D 5, D 6, D 8
Strengthening exercises: K 6, K 7, K 8, K 10

5. The Front Upper Arm Muscles

This muscle group is also referred to as the biceps (two-headed upper arm muscle). Its primary function is to bend the arm at the elbow joint. Its antagonist (the triceps) is the rear upper arm muscle, whose main function is to extend the arm at the elbow joint. Strengthening the biceps has an effect on the punching power of uppercuts, for example. Balanced training of the front and rear muscles of the upper arm is important to avoid disproportionate development.

Stretching exercises: D 3, D 4
Strengthening exercises: K 18, K 19, K 20

6. The Rear Upper Arm Muscles

This muscle group is also known as the triceps (three-headed upper arm muscle). Its primary function is to extend the arm at the elbow joint (antagonist to the front muscles of the upper arm, the biceps). Training the rear muscles of the upper arm increases punching power— for example, in straight punches.

Stretching exercises: D 7, D 8
Strengthening exercises: K 21, K 22, K 23

7. The Abdominal Muscles

This muscle group is important for posture. Its primary functions are the stabilization of the spine as well as the turning and bending of the body. It is the antagonist to the stretching muscles of the back. Strong abdominal muscles are required to withstand the opponent's hits to the body. Frequent training of the abdominal muscles is essential, as their power decreases quickly. In addition, the abdominal muscles and the muscles of the back must have a balanced relationship; therefore, subsequent to the training of the abdominal muscles, the lower muscles of the back must also be strengthened.

Stretching exercises: D 11, D 12, D 13
Strengthening exercises: K 24, K 25, K 26, K 27, K 28, K 29, K 30

8. The Lower Back Muscles

This muscle group runs in two cords from the hip bones along the spine. Its primary functions are to stabilize the spine and to raise the body from a bent position (antagonist to the abdominal muscles). Regular training improves the ability to withstand attacks and prevents injuries. Balanced strengthening of the back and abdomen is required. If the abdominal muscles are neglected, the back contracts into a hollow back, resulting in tension and pain.

Stretching exercises: D 10, D 11, D 13, D 28
Strengthening exercises: K 15, K 16, K 17

9. The Front Thigh Muscles

This muscle group is also known as the quadriceps. Its primary function is extending the leg through the knee joint. Together with the rear muscles of the thigh, it stabilizes the knee joint. Regular training increases kicking power—for example, in front kicks. It is essential to strengthen both the front and rear muscles of the thigh, so that both groups are kept in balance and the knee is best protected.

Stretching exercises: D 15, D 16, D 17
Strengthening exercises: K 31, K 33, K 34, K 35, K 36

10. The Rear Thigh Muscles

The back of the thigh comprises three muscles (hamstring), which extend from the hip (ischium) to the calf. Their primary functions are bending the knee (antagonist to the front muscles of the thigh) and raising the pelvis. In many individuals, these muscles have been shortened because of the number of activities done in a sitting position. Martial arts tends to strengthen the front thigh muscles more than the rear thigh muscles, which can make you more prone to injuries such as knee complaints and torn ligaments. Regular stretching and strengthening of the rear thigh muscles prevent these problems.

Stretching exercises: D 18, D 19, D 20, D 25, D 26, D 30
Strengthening exercises: K 37, K 38, K 39

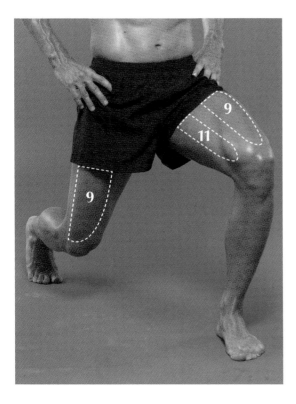

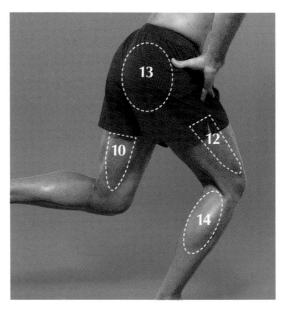

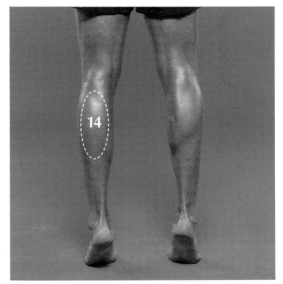

11. The Inner Thigh Muscles

This area comprises the muscles at the inner side of the thigh, which are also referred to as the adductors. Their primary function is to draw in the leg. In addition, as the antagonist to the outer thigh muscles (abductors), they stabilize the standing leg and prevent the body from dropping down while in the straddle stance. Due to this stabilizing function, it is necessary to strengthen these muscles. However, the outer thigh muscles must also be exercised, so that these two muscle groups remain balanced. The adductors are frequently shortened, which is why they must be stretched intensively prior to martial arts training.

Stretching exercises: D 21, D 22, D 26, D 27, D 28, D 29
Strengthening exercises: K 40, K 41

12. The Outer Thigh Muscles

This area comprises the muscles running from the outside of the pelvis across the outside of the thigh to the knee. These muscles are also referred to as the abductors. Their main function is to spread the leg and to stabilize the standing leg (antagonist to the inner thigh muscles, the adductors). The abductors must be exercised regularly, as they tend to weaken. Training these muscles improves kicking power—for example, for side kicks. In addition, it serves to prevent injuries to the knees and makes it easier to absorb leg kicks.

Stretching exercises: D 23, D 24
Strengthening exercises: K 42, K 43

13. The Gluteus Muscles

This muscle group is composed of the gluteus maximus, medius, and minimus. Their main function is controlling the hip joint—for example, when going up a staircase. They also participate in the drawing in and spreading of the leg. The training of the gluteals also has an impact on kicking power, particularly in side kicks and back kicks.

Stretching exercises: D 23, D 24
Strengthening exercises: K 31, K 32, K 33, K 34, K 35

14. The Calf Muscles

This area comprises two cords along the inside and outside of the calf. The primary function of the calf muscles is to generate power from the heel for walking, running, and jumping and the stabilization of the standing foot. In addition, they participate in the bending of the knee joint. Regular training of the calf muscles enables a powerful movement of the heel off the ground, by which many martial arts techniques are started. In addition, they balance the standing leg during kicking sequences. Many people have shortened calf muscles.

Stretching exercises: D 14, D 18, D 25
Strengthening exercises: K 44, K 45

CHAPTER 3

The Training Diet

Proper nutrition is a prerequisite for optimal performance in training and competition and development of the desired body shape. The more optimum and healthy your diet, tailored to your consumption requirements, the better your training results will be. If you consume more food than required by your body, fat deposits will develop. On the other hand, if you have deficits in your food intake, you will not develop any muscles, you will feel weak and tired, and you will be susceptible to infectious diseases. Therefore, it is necessary to find the appropriate balance for the food program. To this end, new findings and many contradictory opinions are continuously publicized. These opinions are frequently accompanied by recommendations that do not take into account the unique needs of each individual. Each person's daily consumption of nutrients depends on the type of activity they will engage in and the basic requirements of the body. Furthermore, each body reacts somewhat differently.

You will attain the best results with a conscious diet. Pay attention to your body's reaction to changes in your diet. The following pages are dedicated to proven nutritional principles, which should serve as the basis for your individual combination of nutrients.

Nutritional Components

Irrespective of the food we consume, the metabolic process (the conversion process in the body) will convert the nutrients contained in the food, so that it can be provided as energy and for the development of endogenous tissue. Carbohydrates, protein, fat, vitamins, mineral substances, and water are nutrients utilized by the body. Carbohydrates and fat primarily provide the energy supply. Protein is mainly used as a constituent of the body. The primary function of the vitamins and mineral substances is the regulation of the metabolic process. The water transports the substances inside the body and regulates the body's temperature.

The optimum diet plan varies among individuals. It derives from the amount and type of physical activity, the amount of muscles, and body height. One guideline for the basic food requirement is that the share of carbohydrates should be approximately 60 percent, fat about 30 percent, and protein about 10 percent. This also applies to martial arts athletes, except that the amount of protein should slightly exceed the recommended percentage. This is particularly important for the development of muscles for a higher fight weight and also for the reduction of fat as a means to step down to a lower weight class. For martial arts athletes the following guidelines can be recommended: share of carbohydrates approximately 55 percent, protein 12–18 percent, and fat 27–33 percent.

Food packages usually indicate the combination of nutrients. It makes sense to check these occasionally to gain a better understanding of what you eat. However, ensuring consumption of an exact combination of the nutrients in accordance with the set guidelines is very time-consuming and, thus, not essential for amateur athletes.

Carbohydrates	→	Generation of energy
Protein	→	Basic body nutrient
Fat	→	Energy generation and storage
Vitamins	→	Regulation of the metabolic process, immune system
Mineral substances	→	Regulation of the metabolic process
Water	→	Transport of body substances, regulation of body temperature

Carbohydrates

Carbohydrates comprise sugar and sugar compounds that form as basic nutrients the most important source of energy for the organism. We differentiate between simple short-chain carbohydrates and complex long-chain carbohydrates. The simple carbohydrates are quickly supplied to the body. They are converted and used just as quickly, which leads to a strong desire for more food. However, the organism requires more time for the conversion of complex carbohydrates. The energy is slowly supplied to the body, so that the complex carbohydrates have a satiating effect over an extended period of time. Simple carbohydrates can be found, for example, in sweets and lemonade; complex carbohydrates in noodles, bread, rice, and potatoes.

Highly nutritious complex carbohydrates—such as whole-grain bread, rice, and noodles—are recommended. The share of carbohydrates in highly nutritious food is, indeed, not any higher than in junk food; however, highly nutritious food contains a higher share of vitamins and mineral substances. Highly nutritious food satisfies longer. For this reason, you should consume highly nutritious food as much as possible, rather than junk food. However, ensure that you change your eating habits slowly, as the body must first get used to the digestion of highly nutritious carbohydrates. Do not make any extensive sudden changes to your diet, particular just prior to a competitive fight, as this may have a negative effect on your performance.

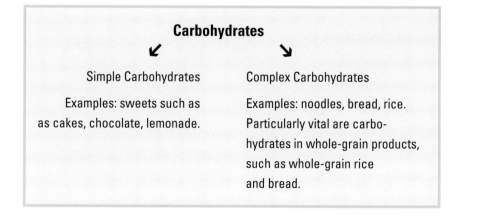

Carbohydrates

Simple Carbohydrates

Examples: sweets such as
as cakes, chocolate, lemonade.

Complex Carbohydrates

Examples: noodles, bread, rice.
Particularly vital are carbohydrates in whole-grain products,
such as whole-grain rice
and bread.

If the carbohydrate intake is greater than the body's use of carbohydrates, the body will store the excess carbohydrates as fat deposits. In the process, the conversion will burn a considerable part of the carbohydrates. Intensive daily training permits the consumption of large amounts of highly nutritious carbohydrates. Careful monitoring of daily consumption is necessary only if you must reduce your weight to meet the requirements of a certain weight division.

Protein

Proteins are the basic nutrients of the body. Skin, muscles, hair, tendons, and ligaments are made up of protein compounds. Proteins are continuously produced, reduced, and changed in the organism. They are necessary for the repair of the body cells, and for the strengthening of muscles and the immune system.

Proteins are made up of different amino acids. Ten essential amino acids must be supplied to the body. The body is able to produce thirteen amino acids by itself, called nonessential amino acids. Many proteins are contained in fish and milk products. There is usually much protein in red meat; however, red meat frequently contains much fat.

If too much protein is consumed, the organism converts it into fat or, in the case of a lack of carbohydrates, into glucose. The body must have a daily supply of protein; otherwise, it will convert muscle protein, which reduces the muscles.

Fats

Fats are concentrated energy suppliers and are, as with all other nutrients, vital for the body. The quality of the fat can be determined by the fatty acids it contains. Accordingly, we differentiate between saturated, simple unsaturated, and polyunsaturated fatty acids. Fatty acids should be reduced as much as possible, as their frequent consumption has a negative effect on the blood lipids and can lead to an increase in cholesterol levels. Saturated fatty acids can be identified by their solid consistency at room temperature—for example, butter and bacon.

From a health point of view, fats, such as those used for deep-frying, are of particular concern.

However, simple unsaturated fatty acids and polyunsaturated fatty acids are indispensable. These fats must be supplied to the body, as it is unable to produce these. Simple unsaturated fats can be found, for example, in olive oil and in nuts. Polyunsaturated fats are found, for example, in sunflower oil, safflower oil, and fish. Replace saturated fatty acids with simple unsaturated and polyunsaturated fatty acids. For example, margarine and butter used in the preparation of your meals can be substituted with high-quality oil.

Active martial arts athletes require more fat than individuals who do not have to exert themselves in sports or work. Nevertheless, they do not have to consciously increase the amount of fat in their diet. This can be explained by the training efforts, which require a higher intake of protein and, frequently, carbohydrates. In the process, the amount of fat will also increase, as the majority of food items include fats. Therefore, the athlete should concentrate on consuming sufficient protein and a large amount of complex carbohydrates.

To lose weight, and thus to be able to compete in a lower weight division, the athlete must attain a negative caloric balance on a regular basis. To this end, the amount of fat in the diet must be reduced to a minimum, provided the athlete has not yet achieved a proportion of body fat below 8 percent. If, on the other hand, the athlete reduces

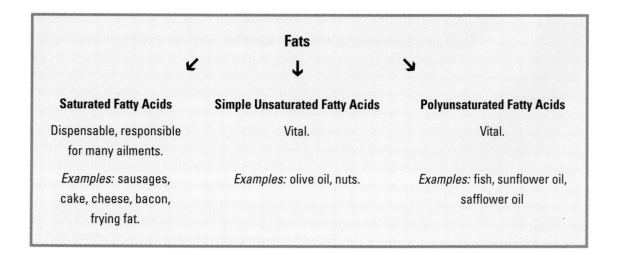

Fats

Saturated Fatty Acids	Simple Unsaturated Fatty Acids	Polyunsaturated Fatty Acids
Dispensable, responsible for many ailments.	Vital.	Vital.
Examples: sausages, cake, cheese, bacon, frying fat.	*Examples:* olive oil, nuts.	*Examples:* fish, sunflower oil, safflower oil

the amount of carbohydrates, he or she will feel weak and tired. A reduction in the amount of protein has a negative effect on the muscles, and the athlete will have less power to carry out his or her techniques.

Vitamins

Vitamins are organic compounds that participate in many metabolic processes and protect the immune system. Minor changes to the body's vitamin content can have far-reaching consequences. Vitamin C, for example, supports our immune system, which is why a higher dose of vitamin C is recommended to fight a cold and for a significant increase in training intensity. Higher doses of some other vitamins, however, have negative effects. Against this backdrop, you should be careful which vitamin compounds you choose from the many that are available.

As far as possible you should eat fruits from your region that have been harvested ripe, as these fruits carry the highest amount of vitamins. The vitamin content of imported fruits is lower, because they are harvested early and must be delivered over long distances. It is not a problem if you consume only a few vitamins on one particular day, provided this does not become the rule. Of vital importance for the vitamin balance is consumption over several days. Return to fresh fruits the next day.

Mineral Substances

Mineral substances influence the growth of bones and many metabolic processes, such as regulating the water balance in the body. Mineral substances include, for example, sodium, potassium, calcium, and magnesium. Mineral substances less present in the body—the so-called trace elements—are, among others, iron, fluorine, zinc, selenium, and iodine. Mineral substances have no performance-enhancing effect. Therefore, it is not sensible to take higher amounts of mineral substances than for a normal physical workload. The necessary normal amount of mineral substances is contained in a balanced diet.

If you have an intensive training program for a number of weeks, food supplements can be sensible, as a lack of mineral substances will have a negative effect on the body. A lack of magnesium, for example, leads to cramps and a lack of zinc will make you susceptible to infections. Against this backdrop, you should pay attention to a sufficient supply of magnesium and zinc if you decide to increase the amount of training significantly.

Water

The human body contains 50–70 percent water. Water is the transport medium of nutrients and regulates the body temperature by the release of sweat. Heat is released by the evaporation of sweat on the skin's surface. Training increases the body temperature, which increases the perspiration. The amount depends on the intensity of training, the ambient temperature, and the humidity.

You should drink a minimum of eight glasses of fluids per day. It is best to drink mineral water. Beverages containing caffeine and alcohol are not suitable to maintain the water balance, as they cause the body to secrete more water. The amount of sweat clearly increases due to the intensive physical strain in martial arts and fitness training. Drink plenty of fluids during training sessions; otherwise, the body will be in danger of dehydration. Along with the sweat, mineral substances will also be secreted, which is why it is best to drink mineral water.

✖ Drink sufficient amounts of water during training.

Dietary Advice for Martial Arts and Fitness Training

Nutritional Basis

Plan your food intake in line with your training targets. Exact monitoring is very time-consuming and, therefore, is unreasonable to expect for amateur athletes. However, some guidelines should be heeded. It is also worthwhile to check the nutritional ingredients on the food packages. This provides you with an overview of your food intake, and you can correct your diet if the desired training results are not achieved. It can be worth the effort for a professional athlete to keep a journal of all food intake.

The major part of the diet should be complex carbohydrates, contained in, for example, potatoes, noodles, and bread. Eat as many whole-grain products as possible. As much as possible, stay away from simple sugar, as contained in sweets, which satiates only for short periods, followed by increased hunger attacks. The amount of carbohydrate-rich food that is suited for your requirements depends on your physical activities and training targets. If you are satisfied with the proportion of fat in your body and you feel fit in training, you have found the appropriate diet. If, however, you wish to reduce the proportion of fat in your body, first try to cut down on the consumption of saturated fatty acids before you start to reduce the supply of carbohydrates.

For your protein, use low-fat products like cottage cheese, tuna, and lean beef. Whey also has a very high proportion of protein and is very low in fat. Whey can be obtained as powder at health food stores and in some pharmacies. Whey is of particular importance for increasing the muscle mass of advanced athletes.

Pay attention to a low-fat diet. Saturated fatty acids should be avoided. Insofar as possible, stay away from products such as sausages, fatty cheese and meat, butter, bacon, and margarine, as these frequently contain a high degree of saturated fatty acids. In addition, you should avoid the consumption of fats used in deep-fat fryers.

However, simple unsaturated fatty acids and polyunsaturated fatty acids are indispensable. Eat plenty of fish and nuts and use high-quality oil, such as sunflower oil, canola oil, and olive oil.

Our food contains many different ingredients, and you must pay attention to a diversified diet. Eat fruit and vegetables on a daily basis and keep changing the products. For example, one day eat an apple, some raspberries, a salad with onions, radishes, and tomatoes. The next day eat a pear, a piece of melon, a carrot, and a large piece of turnip. This way your body obtains all vital vitamins and mineral substances. Should this not be possible, or you dislike large portions of uncooked food, turn to food supplements in the form of vitamin and mineral prod-

ucts. An intensive training program and weight reduction can also increase the body's need for such compounds. In this context, particular attention should be paid to the supply of vitamin C, magnesium, calcium, zinc, and selenium.

Drink plenty of fluids, a minimum of eight glasses a day. If you perspire much, work out hard, or are on a low-calorie diet, you must drink considerably more. Best suited is water, as it contains no calories. However, alcoholic beverages are not suitable for maintenance of the fluid balance, as they cause excessive urination and a greater loss of fluid. They also have a negative influence on the organism and do not supply any nutrients. Therefore, they should be consumed only in moderation, if at all.

✖ You should drink low-fat milk, as the fat content of whole milk is more than twice as high. Based on the daily consumption of milk, a large amount of fat can be reduced.

Regular Meals

Eat at regular intervals. Three main meals are recommended: breakfast, lunch, and dinner. Eat a small snack between breakfast and lunch, and another small snack in the afternoon. Dinner should best be planned for the early evening, so that you can have another small snack after two to three hours. Fruits, vegetables, and protein are recommended for snacks. Sweets should be avoided, as you will soon be hungry again.

The optimum composition of your main meals depends on your lifestyle, your training targets, and your training timetable. Conscious control of your eating habits will show what is good for you. Changes in nutrition should be carried out incrementally and should not be radical. In this way you are able to determine how your body reacts to the changes.

No Low-Calorie Diets

There are many publicized diets that are meant to assist you in attaining the desired weight promptly. These diets can also appear to be attractive to martial arts athletes. However, the inherent reduction in the supply of food causes the body to start saving energy and to change the metabolic process. The body requires protein for the maintenance, strengthening, and regeneration of the body. If the body receives insufficient protein because of the reduced food supply, it will turn to the muscle protein for conversion. This will have a negative effect on the body's muscle–fat ratio. The body will also tire due to the reduced energy intake and will become susceptible to infectious diseases and injuries.

The results of a radical weight-reduction diet are that water will be secreted and muscle mass will be reduced. The desired weight can thus be achieved in a few days. The athlete is now able to compete in a lower weight division; however, a great deal of athletic performance is lost due to decreased stamina and power.

If you resume your normal eating habits after a diet, your weight will rapidly increase. The body stores much of its energy in deposits of fat as a precaution against future food shortages. You will quickly regain your old weight with the same amount of food; your weight may even increase because the basic energy conversion of the body has been reduced due to the decrease in muscles. This phenomenon is the so-called "yo-yo effect," which has caused despair in many dieters. For a martial arts athlete it means that it will become even more difficult to attain the desired weight before the next fight.

You can succeed in the reduction of your body fat only if you train regularly and consume healthy and appropriate food, which will result in a negative calorie balance.

Nutrition Prior to, During, and After Training and Competition

Prior to a training session you can eat a snack rich in carbohydrates—for example, whole-grain muesli or a banana. Abstain from fatty food for at least two hours before training. During training you must drink plenty of fluids, at least two glasses of fluid for each hour of training. Drink water or a mixed drink containing two-thirds water and one-third apple juice (not apple-flavored fruit juice). After training you must first refuel with carbohydrates.

In the course of martial arts tournaments the athletes must compete several times. Here it makes sense to eat small food items rich in carbohydrates between the contests—for example, carbohydrate bars and sports drinks enriched with carbohydrates.

As a matter of principle, it is better to have several meals spread throughout the day than to have one main meal. This is a basic requirement for successful muscle training. Eat several meals containing protein throughout the day and do not attempt to obtain your full requirement of protein in one meal. Apply the same principle to the consumption of protein compounds.

An increase in the size of muscles is possible only through increased food consumption. In the process, attention must be paid to products low in fat. Otherwise, the risk is that the athlete will not only increase muscle size, but also the proportion of fat. As a result, the athlete may face a better-trained opponent in a higher weight division. An exception is the super heavyweight division, which has no upper limit. It is only in this case that the athlete's proportion of fat is not of decisive importance (see pp. 205–212).

Protein Supply

It is important to check the diet's supply of protein, at least from time to time. In this context it must be ensured that protein is consumed at several meals and that it consists of different food items. Only in this way can it be certain that the body absorbs and converts the protein and that it contains the required amino acids.

The following are general guidelines. Each body has a different composition, particularly the muscles, and reacts differently to food intake.

Training Target: Maintaining the Weight Class
Recommended daily supply of protein: approximately 3.5 g per pound of body weight; at least 2.5 g per pound of body weight.

Training Target: Reduction of Body Fat for Lower Weight Division
Recommended daily supply of protein: 3.5–4.5 g per pound of body weight. However, if the muscles have been built up extensively, increase the supply of protein even more.

Training Target: Increase of Muscle Size for Higher Weight Division
Recommended daily supply of protein: approximately 4.5 g per pound of body weight. The amount increases in accordance with the size of muscles previously built up. Professional bodybuilders consume up to 8.5 g of protein per pound of body weight.

Part II: Flexibility Training Exercises

CHAPTER **4**

Introduction

Because a flexible body is essential for the delivery of technically demanding martial arts techniques, stretching is a must prior to each martial arts training session. The trainer usually demonstrates a stretching program, which you can adopt for training at home. You should also stretch your body before and after each stamina and power training session. In this way you prepare your body for the demands of training. In addition, you reduce the risk of injuries and accelerate the regeneration phase.

The term *stretching* describes the deliberate execution of exercises aimed at improved flexibility. In this book it means the slow positioning of your body until you experience a slight stretch stimulus in the muscles. You then reduce the stretch stimulus and improve flexibility by executing the "relaxing–extending" or "tensing–relaxing–extending" stretching methods (see pp. 35–37).

Part II will advise you on the basics of stretching and the most important exercises. If you develop a stretching program based on these exercises, include at least one stretching session for each muscle group (see pp. 10–17). To reduce the preparation time required before stamina and power training, stretch only those specific muscle groups that you will concentrate on during your subsequent training.

CHAPTER **5**

Stretching Methods

The stretching exercises described in this book can be carried out as "relaxing–extending" and "tensing–relaxing–extending." Test both variants and use the method that facilitates your muscle relaxation best in the long run. Both methods are effective. However, the one best for you depends on your own experience. From time to time you should try the other variant again.

"Relaxing–Extending" Method

The "relaxing–extending" stretching method was made popular by Bob Anderson. Stretching is divided into two phases: easy stretching and progressive stretching (see Anderson 1996, pp. 8–12). Focus on regular breathing during the exercises, concentrate on the muscles to be stretched, and ensure that these are relaxed.

In the *first stretching phase,* carefully take a position in which you experience a minor stretch stimulus. Maintain the position for a few seconds and consciously relax the muscle. Different opinions exist on the exact length of time. My advice to untrained athletes is to count silently up to 20 seconds while maintaining the position. As with progressive stretching, act in accordance with your own physical sensation and not with the length of time. The stretch tension should decrease somewhat after a short time period. Even though you may not feel the decrease, you should feel comfortable in the position and be able to relax. Should this not be the case, you must relax slightly and decrease the tension.

In the *second stretching phase,* intensify the position until you experience a renewed stimulus. Maintain the new position for about 20 seconds. The extended position must also be experienced as comfortable; otherwise, it must be corrected.

At the end, carefully move out of the stretch.

Execution of Stretching

1. Move the muscle slowly into a position in which you experience a slight stretch stimulus.
2. Maintain the position for approximately 20 seconds (first phase).
3. Extend the stretch until you experience new tension. Maintain this position for approximately 20 seconds as well (second phase).
4. Move carefully out of the stretch.

"Tensing–Relaxing–Extending" Method

This stretching method can be used by advanced athletes, who have already developed a comprehensive understanding of their muscles. Similar variants with recommended times exist; the combination of this method with other methods can be used in the rehabilitation of sports injuries, for example. Years of experience have proved the following stretching method to be the most effective for me and many of my training partners in the areas of martial arts and fitness.

The "tensing–relaxing–extending" method is particularly suited for shortened and cramped muscles. Competitive athletes use it frequently to improve their flexibility. Experienced athletes can also use the method to shorten the warm-up phase in training, as the tension increases the blood flow, thereby warming the muscles. Use this method very carefully after training to avoid cramps.

In the *first stretching phase,* slowly move into a position in which you feel a minor stretch tension. Tense the muscle to be stretched with medium intensity against an obstacle and do not change the position. Depending on the starting position, the obstacle can be a wall, the floor, or a training partner. The tension can also be applied to an imaginary obstacle. Different opinions exist as to how long and with what intensity tensing should be carried out. For example, one opinion is that the tensing should be carried out with full intensity for 1–2 seconds. However, this entails too high of a risk of injury; furthermore, it is difficult to fully activate the muscle in such a short period. I recommend a tensing period of about 5 seconds with medium intensity. Then relax the muscle for approximately 1–3 seconds. The exact period depends on the time you require for relaxation.

In the *second stretching phase,* intensify the position until you experience a new stimulus. Briefly maintain that position before you again tense the muscle to be stretched, and relax for extension of the position. The procedure should be carried out at least once, but it can also be repeated additional times. The extension of the stretch position will decrease with each exercise, until nearly no extension is discerned.

Execution of Stretching

1. Move the muscle slowly into a position in which you experience slight tension.
2. Tense the muscle to be stretched with medium intensity against a real or imaginary obstacle for about 5 seconds, without change of the joint position (first phase).
3. Relax the muscle for about 1–3 seconds, without changing your position.
4. Extend the stretch until you experience a new stimulus, and maintain this stance for a few seconds (second phase).
5. Repeat the first phase.
6. Carefully move out of the stretch.

Tensing the Muscle Groups

Pay attention to exactly where you feel the stretch tension. Tense the stimulated muscle group in the opposite direction from which the body is moved. Do not move the joint. If you move the body in the direction of the starting position, it will subsequently be impossible to achieve an extension of the stretch position.

CHAPTER **6**

Rules for Stretching

Warming up is required prior to intensive stretching (see pp. 193–195). To decrease the tension of specific muscles—for example, due to desk work—you can also stretch without prior warm-up.

Get into a stable starting position, so that you can fully concentrate on stretching. It is particularly at a high stretch intensity that an unstable stance can allow you to exceed the optimum position, resulting in injury.

Find the correct stretch position by moving slowly and carefully. Rapid moves can lead to injuries. Then move away from the stretch position just as carefully.

Your performance level determines the stretch position. Do not attempt to copy the same stretch position as your training partner or as depicted in this book, but let yourself be guided by your own perception, as each individual has different physical preconditions. You will also realize that the tension of your muscles differs from day to day. Never try to achieve a stretch position by force. Once you experience pain, the stretch position must be decreased promptly; otherwise, the muscle will continue to harden and not relax. Your flexibility will improve only if you accustom the relaxed muscle slowly to the new stretch position, and if this is carried out regularly.

Once you have found the correct stretch position, concentrate on the muscle to be stretched. Relax the muscle ("relaxing–extending" stretching method) or apply tension before you relax ("tensing- relaxing-extending" stretching method).

Breathe slowly and regularly during the relaxation process and pay attention to the relaxation in the muscle. Exhale during the extension of the stretch position.

To maintain your flexibility in the long run, you must stretch regularly. Stretch at least twice a week and avoid lengthy breaks between stretch days. There is no minimum period between stretch days, as stretching regenerates the body and causes no physical strain.

CHAPTER 7

Stretching Exercises for the Upper Body

This chapter describes the most important stretching exercises for the upper body. Start your stretch program by first removing the tension in your neck area. This will help you to adapt yourself to the stretch program.

The muscle groups on the following pages are arranged according to the recommended training process. Some of the muscle groups have been combined for better clarity. More detailed information about the muscle groups appears on pages 10–17.

Execution of the Exercises

The arrows on the exercise photos show the direction of the move. In the starting position, take the stance in which you experience a minor stretch stimulus. Now apply one of the two previously introduced stretching methods: "relaxing–extending" or "tensing-relaxing-extending" (see pp. 35–37). Tensing the muscles in the "tensing-relaxing-extending" method must be carried out opposite to the direction of the move.

Although an exercise is described for only one side of the body, both sides of the body should always be stretched.

The description of the exercises indicates whether the stretching is of primary (++) or secondary (+) importance for the muscles.

> **The neck muscles**
>
> **The chest muscles and the front upper arm muscles**
>
> **The shoulder muscles and the rear upper arm muscles**
>
> **The lower and upper back muscles**
>
> **The abdominal muscles**

The Neck Muscles

D 1: Leaning the Head Sideways

> Stretching:
> ++ Neck muscles

Starting Position

Stand upright with your head lowered toward the right side. Slowly lower your left arm, until you experience a minor stretch stimulus in the left side of your neck. Avoid raising the left shoulder.

Relaxing–Extending

Maintain this position and relax your muscles. In the process, breathe regularly. Once the stretch tension lessens after a few seconds, raise the right hand to the top of the head and pull your head down with the palm of the hand until you experience a new stimulus.

Tensing–Relaxing–Extending

Raise your right hand to the top of the head. Tense the left-hand side of your head against the palm of the hand and do not change the head position. Then release the tension and briefly relax the tensed muscles. Finally, pull the head farther down to the right. Avoid raising the left shoulder in the process.

Variant

You can reach different parts of the neck muscles if you do not lower the left arm but pull it in a bent position along the back.

D 2: Pushing the Head to the Front

Stretching:
++ Neck muscles

Starting Position

Take an upright stance and slowly lower the head to the front until you experience a minor stretch stimulus in the neck muscles. At the same time, pull the shoulders slightly down toward the back.

Relaxing–Extending

Maintain the position and relax your muscles. In the process, continue to breathe regularly. Once the stretch tension decreases, after a few seconds, push the head farther down until you feel a new stimulus.

Tensing–Relaxing–Extending

Tense the back of the head against the palms of the hands while not changing your position. Then release the tension and briefly relax the tensed muscles. Finally, push the head farther down.

The Chest Muscles and the Front Upper Arm Muscles

D 3: Pushing the Chest Forward

Stretching: ++ Chest muscles   + Front upper arm and front shoulder muscles

Starting Position

Start with a lunge step. Raise your arms in a U-shape. Push the chest forward and simultaneously move your arms to the rear until you experience a minor stretch stimulus.

Relaxing–Extending

Maintain the position and consciously relax the muscles. Continue to breathe regularly. Once the stretch tension decreases, after a few seconds, slightly push the chest farther forward until you experience a new stimulus.

Tensing–Relaxing–Extending

Tense your arms against an imaginary obstacle to the front, while not moving your arms forward. Then release the tension and briefly relax the tensed muscles. Finally, move the chest somewhat farther to the front.

Variant

If you maintain your arms in an extended position, you intensify the stretch of the front upper arm muscles.

D 4: Lateral Arm Rest

> **Stretching:**
> ++ Chest muscles
> + Front upper arm and front shoulder muscles

Starting Position

Kneel on the floor and rest one arm sideways insofar as possible. The other bent arm supports the upper body. The thighs are in a nearly vertical position. Lower the shoulder until you experience a minor stretch stimulus. The position of the thighs is not changed in the process.

Relaxing–Extending

Maintain the position and consciously relax the muscles. Continue to breathe regularly. Once the stretch tension decreases, after a few seconds, lower the shoulder somewhat farther until you experience a new stimulus.

Tensing–Relaxing–Extending

Tense your arm against the floor, while not changing the arm position. Then release the tension and briefly relax the tensed muscles. Finally, slightly lower the shoulder even farther.

Variant

If you rest the arm somewhat lower or higher, you stretch different parts of the chest muscles.

The exercise can also be carried out in a standing position: Press your arm against a wall or a high object. Then turn your upper body forward until you experience a stretch stimulus.

The Shoulder Muscles and the Rear Upper Arm Muscles

D 5: Lateral Arm Push to the Rear

> Stretching:
> ++ Lateral and rear shoulder muscles
> + Rear upper arm and upper back muscles

Starting Position

Stand upright and hold your left arm shoulder-high in front of the body. Seize the left elbow with your right hand, then push the left arm past the head sideways to the back, until you experience a minor stretch stimulus.

Relaxing–Extending

Maintain the position and consciously relax the muscles. Continue to breathe regularly in the process. Once the stretch tension decreases, after a few seconds, push the arm somewhat farther until you experience a new stimulus.

Tensing–Relaxing–Extending

Push your left elbow into the right hand, while not changing the starting position. Then release the tension and briefly relax the tensed muscles. Finally, continue to move the arm somewhat farther.

D 6: Gripping the Shoulder Blades

Stretching:
++ Shoulder muscles
 + Upper back muscles

Starting Position

Stand upright and move your hands crosswise in the direction of the shoulder blades until you experience a minor stretch stimulus. The upper arms remain in a horizontal position. Well-trained athletes take hold of the shoulder blade edges.

Relaxing–Extending

Maintain the position and consciously relax the muscles. Continue to breathe regularly. Once the stretch tension decreases, after a few seconds, proceed, moving your hands slightly until you feel a new stimulus. Advanced athletes then move their hands along the edges of the shoulder blades.

Tensing–Relaxing–Extending

Stretch the shoulder blades apart without changing the position of the arms. Then release the tension and briefly relax the tensed muscles. Finally, extend your hands somewhat farther.

Variant

The exercise can be intensified if you pull the shoulder blades forward.

D 7: Pushing the Arm Down Behind the Head

Stretching:
++ Rear upper arm muscles
 + Shoulder and upper back muscles

Starting Position

Stand upright, the left forearm pointing down behind the head, while the upper arm is in a somewhat horizontal position. Place the right hand on the left elbow and push the arm straight down until you experience a minor stretch stimulus.

Relaxing–Extending

Maintain the position and consciously relax the muscles. Continue to breathe regularly. Once the stretch tension decreases, after a few seconds, push the elbow farther down until you feel a new stimulus.

Tensing–Relaxing–Extending

Push the left elbow into the palm of the right hand without changing the arm position. Then release the tension and briefly relax the tensed muscles. Finally, push the elbow farther down.

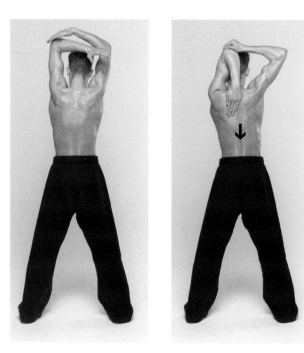

Variant

If you do not move your arm straight down, but diagonally to the right side with a simultaneous move of the upper body in the same direction, you intensify the stretch of the muscles in the upper back.

D 8: Holding Hands Behind the Back

> **Stretching:**
> ++ Shoulder, front and rear upper arm muscles
> + Chest muscles

Starting Position

Stand upright, the left forearm pointing down behind the head, while the upper arm has taken on a somewhat vertical position. Slowly raise the right forearm behind the back until both hands can join.

Relaxing–Extending

Maintain the position and consciously relax the muscles. Continue to breathe regularly. Once the stretch tension decreases, after a few seconds, move the hands closer to each other until you feel a new stimulus.

Tensing–Relaxing–Extending

Stretch the arms apart without changing the arm position. Then release the tension and briefly relax the tensed muscles. Finally, move the hands closer to each other.

Variant

If you can feel a stretch tension before the hands join each other, simplify the exercise by holding a towel stretched between your hands behind the back. Then move the hands along the towel toward each other, so that the distance between them gets shorter, until you reach the intended stretch position.

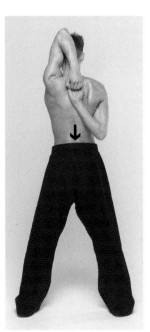

The Lower and Upper Back Muscles

D 9: Arm and Upper Body Stretch

> Stretching:
> + Upper back, abdominal, and shoulder muscles

Starting Position

Stand upright and hold the arms in front of your body, interlocking your fingers. Initially, stretch the arms to the front and turn the palms of your hands away from the body. Then move the stretched arms above your head, moving your head so that you keep eye contact with the fingers. While you are doing this, stretch your body upward until you experience a minor stretch stimulus.

Relaxing–Extending

Maintain the position and consciously relax the muscles. Continue to breathe regularly. Once the stretch tension decreases, after a few seconds, continue stretching the upper body upward until you experience a new stimulus.

Tensing–Relaxing–Extending

Stretch the shoulders toward the floor without lowering the arms. Then release the tension and briefly relax the tensed muscles. Finally, stretch your body farther upward.

Variant

If the stretching of the hands and fingers proves to be too painful, do not turn the palms of your hands outward.

D 10: Bending the Upper Body to the Front

> **Stretching:**
> ++ Lower and upper back muscles
> + Shoulder, neck, and gluteus muscles

Starting Position

Sit on the floor with bent legs. Take hold of the lower legs with your arms from below and slightly move your upper body forward, while moving the hips to the front. Extend the position with a forward motion supported by your hands, until you feel a minor stretch tension.

Relaxing–Extending

Maintain the position and consciously relax the muscles. Continue to breathe regularly. Once the stretch tension decreases, after a few seconds, pull the upper part of your body farther forward until you experience a new stimulus.

Tensing–Relaxing–Extending

Press the arms against the lower legs, and press the back muscles upward without changing the starting position. Then release the tension and briefly relax the tensed muscles. Finally, pull the upper body farther forward.

Variant

The exercise can also be carried out sitting on a chair or in a standing position with bent legs.

D 11: Lateral Bending of the Upper Body

> **Stretching:**
> ++ Lateral abdominal, lower back, and upper back muscles

Starting Position

Stand upright, legs hip-width apart. Stretch one arm up into the air and bend the upper part of your body to the other side until you feel a minor stretch stimulus. Ensure that the upper part of your body remains in one line and that you do not move the hips to the side.

Relaxing–Extending

Maintain the position and consciously relax the muscles. Continue to breathe regularly. Once the stretch tension decreases, after a few seconds, continue bending sideways until you experience a new stimulus.

Tensing–Relaxing–Extending

Grip the wrist of the raised arm with the arm pointing down. Stretch the arms apart without changing the starting position. Then release the tension and briefly relax the tensed muscles. Finally, continue bending the upper part of your body to the side.

Variant

Good control of the exercise is possible if your outer arm above the head holds on to an object—for example, wall bars. Slowly move your hip to the outside, away from the wall bars, until you feel a slight stretch stimulus.

The Abdominal Muscles

D **12**: Prone Abdominal Stretch

Stretching:
++ Abdominal muscles

Starting Position

You are in a prone position on the floor. Your hands are resting on the floor, shoulder-width apart, in front of the head, and your upper body is down. Slightly stretch your arms and raise the upper body until you feel a slight stretch stimulus in the abdominal muscles.

Relaxing–Extending

Maintain the position and consciously relax the muscles. Continue to breathe regularly. Once the stretch tension decreases, after a few seconds, raise your upper body farther until you experience a new stimulus.

Tensing–Relaxing–Extending

Press the hands against the floor without changing the position of your upper body. Then release the tension and briefly relax the tensed muscles. Finally, continue to raise your body.

Following the stretch, slowly lower the upper body back to the floor.

Variant

Untrained athletes can use the forearms, instead of stretched arms, for support.

Training athletes with back problems should consult their doctor for advice prior to the exercise.

D **13**: Bending the Legs to the Side

Stretching:
++ Lateral abdominal and lower back muscles
 + Upper back muscles

Starting Position

Lie on your back with your arms extending backward above your head, and the legs bent at the knees, with the feet on the floor. Move your legs to one side until you experience a minor stretch stimulus.

Relaxing–Extending

Maintain the position and consciously relax the muscles. Continue to breathe regularly. Once the stretch tension decreases, after a few seconds, move your knee farther toward the floor until you feel a new stimulus.

Tensing–Relaxing–Extending

Press the upper body down and the knees against each other without changing the starting position. Then release the tension and briefly relax the tensed muscles. Finally, move the knee farther toward the floor.

Variant

Intensify the exercise by pulling the feet closer to the upper body.

CHAPTER 8

Stretching Exercises for the Legs and Buttocks

This chapter is dedicated to the most important stretching exercises for the legs and buttocks. Arrange a program to initially stretch only the calf muscles, as these are also stretched in many exercises and their tightness should not hinder other stretches. Then concentrate on the exercises for the muscles of the front and rear thigh. Finally, stretch the inner and outer muscles of the thigh and the buttocks.

The muscle groups on the following pages are arranged according to the recommended training process. Some have been combined for reasons of clarity. More details on the muscle groups are found on pages 10–17.

Execution of the Exercises

The arrows on the exercise photos show the direction of moves. In the starting position, take a position in which you experience a minor stretch stimulus. Now apply one of the two described stretching methods: "relaxing-extending" or "tensing-relaxing-extending" (see pp. 35–37). Tensing the muscles in the "tensing- relaxing-extending" method must be carried out opposite to the direction of the move.

Although an exercise is described for only one side of the body, both sides of the body should always be stretched.

The description of the exercises indicates whether the stretching is of primary (++) or secondary (+) importance for the muscles.

> **The calf muscles**
>
> **The front thigh muscles**
>
> **The rear thigh muscles**
>
> **The inner thigh muscles**
>
> **The outer thigh muscles and the gluteus muscles**

The Calf Muscles

D 14: Calf Stretch Alternating Between Straight and Bent Leg

Stretching:
++ Calf muscles

Starting Position

From a straight stance, take a medium step to the front with the left leg, accompanied by the hip. The feet are straight and point to the front; the rear leg is slightly bent and its heel is raised. Stretch the right leg slightly, and simultaneously push the heel in the direction of the floor until you experience a minor stretch stimulus in the calf muscles.

Relaxing–Extending

Maintain the position and consciously relax the muscles. Continue to breathe regularly. Once the stretch tension decreases, after a few seconds, move the heel somewhat farther away until you can feel a new stimulus.

Tensing–Relaxing–Extending

Choose a starting position so that you can reach the floor with your rear heel. Push the heel against the floor without changing the foot position. Then release the tension and briefly relax the tensed muscles. Finally, bend the front leg somewhat deeper and shift the weight of your body forward, to intensify the stretch position.

   After stretching in the upper position, bend the knee of the stretched leg so as to feel the stretch in the lower area of the calf and in the Achilles tendon. Keep the heel on the ground.

The Front Thigh Muscles

D 15: Bending the Lower Leg

Stretching:
++ Front thigh muscles

Starting Position

Starting in a prone position, with the head resting on the floor, move one leg with its own power as far as possible toward the buttocks. Take hold of the foot and pull it in the direction of the buttocks until you can feel a minor stretch stimulus. In the process, consciously press your hips against the floor. If you cannot get hold of your foot, wrap a towel around the instep and pull your foot with the help of the towel.

Relaxing–Extending

Maintain the position and consciously relax the muscles. Continue to breathe regularly. Once the stretch tension decreases, after a few seconds, pull the foot farther toward the buttocks until you experience a new stimulus. Advanced athletes also raise the knee into the air without changing the hip position.

Tensing–Relaxing–Extending

Press the foot against the holding hand without changing the starting position. Then release the tension and briefly relax the tensed muscles. Finally, pull the foot farther toward you. Advanced athletes also raise the bent knee up into the air.

Variant

The exercise can also be carried out in an upright position or lying sideways on the floor. If you have difficulties maintaining your balance in an upright stance, lean against an object for support.

D 16: Front Thigh Stretch Leaning Back Upper Body

> **Stretching:**
> **++ Front thigh muscles**

Starting Position

Kneel on the floor, the insteps of your feet touching the ground and the knees pointing forward. Keep the upper body upright. Slowly lower your buttocks until they are resting on the heels. If you did not experience a stretch tension so far, carefully lean your upper body back until the stimulus can be felt.

Relaxing–Extending

Maintain the position and consciously relax your muscles. Continue to breathe regularly. Once the stretch tension decreases, after a few seconds, lean your upper body farther back until you experience a new stimulus.

Tensing–Relaxing–Extending

Push the lower legs against the floor without changing the starting position. Then release the tension and briefly relax the tensed muscles. Finally, lean the upper body farther back.

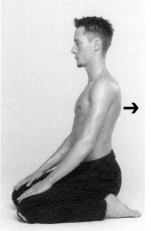

   Movement of the upper body must be carried out slowly and carefully. For safety you can use your hands for support.

Variant

Trained athletes can rest their back on the ground. In this position, particular attention should be paid to regular breathing and complete relaxation.

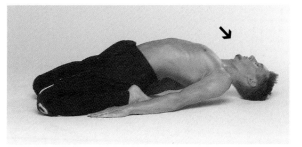

D **17**: Lunge

> Stretching:
> ++ Front thigh muscles

Starting Position

Take a lunge step, and rest the lower leg on the floor. Lower your buttocks as far as possible and turn the front foot so that the instep is lying on the ground. Straighten the upper body and stabilize the position. Relax the hip and move it down to the front until you experience a minor stretch stimulus.

Relaxing–Extending

Maintain the position and consciously relax the muscles. Continue to breathe regularly. Once the stretch tension decreases, after a few seconds, move the hip farther forward until you experience a new stimulus.

Tensing–Relaxing–Extending

Press the rear leg against the ground without changing the foot position. Then release the tension and briefly relax the tensed muscles. Finally, move the hip somewhat farther down.

Subsequently, pull up the rear foot for a more intensive stretch of the front of the thigh. Repeat the exercise as before. The pressure in "tensing-relaxing-extending" is generated by the instep held against the hand.

The Rear Thigh Muscles

D 18: Rear Thigh Stretch Bending Upper Body Forward

> Stretching:
> ++ Rear thigh and back muscles
> + Calf muscles

Starting Position

Stand upright with the feet close to each other and the legs straight. Bending at the waist, slowly move the upper body in the direction of the floor until you experience a minor stretch stimulus.

Relaxing–Extending

Maintain the position and consciously relax the muscles. Continue to breathe regularly. Once the stretch tension decreases, after a few seconds, lower the upper body farther toward the ground until you can feel a new stimulus.

Tensing–Relaxing–Extending

Tense the stretched legs backward and the lower back upward without changing the starting position. Then release the tension and briefly relax the tensed muscles. Finally, bend the upper body farther toward the floor.

Variant

The exercise can be carried out while sitting on the floor with the legs stretched straight in front of you. Move both the hips and the upper body to the front at the same time until you feel a minor stretch stimulus. The movement should be made as if you were pulled forward by the breastbone. Subsequently, pull in the toes for a more intensive stretch of the calf muscles.

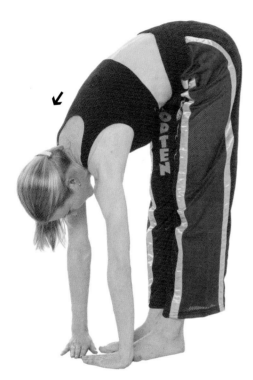

D 19: Stretching the Leg in the Air

> Stretching:
> ++ **Rear thigh muscles**
> + **Gluteus and calf muscles**

Starting Position

Lie on your back and pull one leg toward your body, bending the leg at the knee. Grasp it from the front and continue pulling until you feel a minor stretch stimulus.

The other leg remains on the ground. If you cannot keep it there, you must actively push it down during the entire exercise. In addition, the next training sessions should include particularly intensive stretching of these shortened muscles (D 17).

Relaxing–Extending

Maintain the position and consciously relax the muscles. Continue to breathe regularly. Once the stretch tension decreases, after a few seconds, pull the knee closer to your body until you feel a new stimulus.

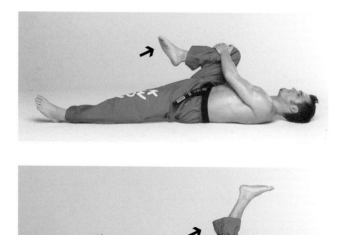

Tensing–Relaxing–Extending

Tense the bent leg against the hands without changing the leg position. Then release the tension and briefly relax the tensed muscles. Finally, pull the knee closer to the body.

Subsequently, lower the leg somewhat and take hold below the hollow behind the knee. Stabilize the knee in this position and raise the lower part of the raised leg until you experience a stretch tension. Then repeat the stretching method used previously.

D 20: Splits to the Front

> **Stretching:**
> ++ Rear thigh and front thigh muscles

Starting Position

Kneel with the left leg on the ground, the right leg stretched straight in front, and the upper body in an upright position. Slowly move the hip together with the right leg to the front until you feel a minor stretch tension. For controlled execution of the exercise you can use the hands for support.

Relaxing–Extending

Maintain the position and consciously relax the muscles. Continue to breathe regularly. Once the stretch tension decreases, after a few seconds, shift the front leg farther forward until you can feel a new stimulus.

Tensing–Relaxing–Extending

Press the legs against the floor without changing the starting position. Then release the tension and briefly relax the tensed muscles. Finally, shift your leg farther to the front.

Variant

Advanced athletes fully extend their stretched legs flat on the ground.

The Inner Thigh Muscles

D 21: Straddle Stand

> **Stretching:**
> ++ Inner thigh muscles
> + Calf and rear thigh muscles

Starting Position

From an upright stance, move the feet out into a straddle position until you experience a minor stretch stimulus. Ensure that the hips remain in front and do not shift backward.

Relaxing–Extending

Maintain the position and consciously relax your muscles. Continue to breathe regularly. Once the stretch tension decreases, after a few seconds, bend one leg until you experience a new stimulus. Remain in this position and repeat the stretching exercise. Then straighten the leg and perform the exercise with the other side.

Tensing–Relaxing–Extending

Tense, pushing the inner legs toward the floor without changing the starting position. Then release the tension and briefly relax the tensed muscles. Bend one leg until you feel a new stimulus. Remain in this position and repeat the stretching exercise. Then straighten the leg and perform the exercise with the other side.

Subsequently, you can move the legs farther apart until you experience a new stretch sensation, and repeat the stretching exercise.

Variant

In the lower position you can shift part of the weight to the hands, thus performing the exercise in a controlled manner.

Very advanced athletes are able to perform the lateral splits and rest the upper body on the floor in front of them.

D 22: Front Bend of the Upper Body from a Straddle Position

Stretching:
++ Inner thigh and back muscles
 + Rear thigh and calf muscles

Starting Position

Sit down, with the legs in a straddle position. Move the arms forward until you feel a minor stretch stimulus. In the process, bend the upper body forward, as if you were pulled by the breastbone, and simultaneously push the hips to the front.

Relaxing–Extending

Maintain the position and consciously relax the muscles. Continue to breathe regularly. Once the stretch tension decreases, after a few seconds, move the upper body farther forward until you experience a new stimulus.

Tensing–Relaxing–Extending

Tense the rear of the legs and the hands against the ground without changing the starting position. Then release the tension and briefly relax the tensed muscles. Finally, proceed moving the upper body farther toward the front.

Subsequently, carry out the exercise to the left and the right side.

The Outer Thigh Muscles and the Gluteus Muscles

D 23: Body Rotation in a Sitting Position

> **Stretching:**
> ++ Gluteus and outer thigh muscles
> + Back muscles

Starting Position

Sit down with your legs stretched straight in front of you, and an upright upper body. Bring the right leg across the left, and position the right foot as close to the buttocks as possible. The sole of the right foot rests on the floor and it points nearly straight to the front. Relax the right leg and pull it toward the body until you experience a minor stretch stimulus. You can pull the leg in with your hands, or just move the foot by itself.

Relaxing–Extending

Maintain the position and consciously relax the muscles. Continue to breathe regularly. Once the stretch tension decreases, after a few seconds, place your left elbow on the outside of the right knee, turn the head and the upper body clockwise until you feel a new stretch stimulus, and repeat the stretch.

Tensing–Relaxing–Extending

Tense by pulling the knee toward the torso with the hands without changing the starting position. Release the tension and briefly relax the tensed muscles. Finally, put your left arm against the outside of the right knee, turn the head and upper body clockwise, and repeat this stretching method.

Variant

The leg resting on the floor can also be bent during the exercise, which enables a more intensive stretching of the upper body.

D 24: Pulling the Foot

> Stretching:
> ++ Gluteus and outer thigh muscles

Starting Position

Sit down with your upper body upright and your legs stretched straight in front of you on the floor. Draw up the right leg, holding the ankle and calf, and hold it with your hands or place it against the left knee. The right knee should move to the outside. Pull your right leg closer to the body until you can feel a minor stretch stimulus.

Relaxing–Extending

Maintain the position and consciously relax the muscles. Continue to breathe regularly. Once the stretch tension decreases, after a few seconds, pull the right lower leg farther toward you until you can feel a new stimulus.

Tensing–Relaxing–Extending

Push your right foot against the hands or the left knee without changing the starting position. Then release the tension and briefly relax the tensed muscles. Finally, pull the right leg farther toward you as described.

Variant

The exercise can also be done lying on the back.

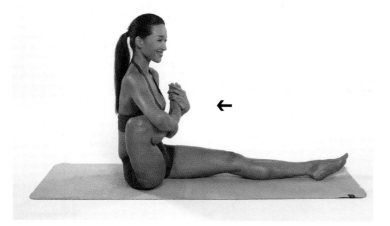

CHAPTER 9

Partner Exercises

Execution of the Exercises

The arrows on the exercise photos show the direction of the movement. To start, take a position in which you experience a minor stretch stimulus. Now apply one of the two described stretching methods: "relaxing–extending" or "tensing–relaxing–extending" (see pp. 35–37). When tensing the muscles in the "tensing–relaxing–extending" method, be sure to tense the muscles being stretched in the direction opposite from the stretch.

Although each exercise is described for only one side of the body, both sides of the body should always be stretched.

The description of the exercises indicates whether the stretching is of primary (++) or secondary (+) importance for the muscles.

D 25: Pushing the Leg Up in a Standing Position

Stretching:
++ Rear thigh muscles
 + Calf muscles and gluteus muscles

Starting Position

Stand upright. Your training partner picks up your leg and brings it upward with one hand; with the other hand, your partner holds both of your hands to stabilize your position. Your partner then bends his or her legs, placing your leg on his or her shoulder then slowly straightening the legs, thus raising your leg at the same time. Continue to keep your upper body erect. As soon as you experience a minor stretch stimulus, tell your partner and remain in this position.

Relaxing–Extending

Maintain the position and consciously relax the muscles. Continue to breathe regularly. Once the stretch tension decreases, after a few seconds, your partner continues to raise your leg until you experience a new stimulus.

Tensing–Relaxing–Extending

Press your lower calf against your partner's shoulder. Your partner remains in the same position so that the starting position remains intact. You then release the tension and briefly relax the tensed muscles. Finally, your partner raises your leg higher.

Variant

Advanced athletes can also bend forward at the waist (keeping the back straight) toward their partner and into the stretch.

D 26: Raising the Leg from Behind

> **Stretching:**
> **++ Inner and rear thigh muscles**

Starting Position

From a standing position, lean your upper body forward. To stabilize your position, hold on to something, like a chair. Stretch one leg straight out behind you with your training partner holding it up, raising your leg until you feel a minor stretch stimulus. Communicate this to your partner and maintain this position.

Relaxing–Extending

Maintain the position and consciously relax the muscles. Continue to breathe regularly. Once the stretch tension decreases, after a few seconds, your partner continues to raise your leg until you feel a new stimulus.

Tensing–Relaxing–Extending

Push your leg against your partner, who remains in the same position to maintain the starting position. For greater stability, he or she can place your leg on his or her shoulder. You then release the tension and briefly relax the tensed muscles. Finally, your partner raises your leg even farther.

D **27**: Outside Push of the Legs in a Straddle Position

> **Stretching:**
> **++ Inner thigh muscles**

Starting Position

Get into a straddle position, your legs stretched out to either side of your torso on the floor. Your training partner positions his or her feet next to the inside of your ankles, with his or her knees bent, and grips your hands or lower arms. Your partner then slowly straightens his or her legs, moving your legs farther to the outside, until you feel a minor stretch stimulus and communicate this to your partner.

Relaxing–Extending

Maintain the position and consciously relax the muscles. Continue to breathe regularly. Once the stretch tension decreases, after a few seconds, your partner pushes your legs farther to the outside until you can feel a new stimulus.

Tensing–Relaxing–Extending

Tense your inner legs against your partner's feet. The partner maintains their position so that your starting position remains intact. You then release the tension and briefly relax the tensed muscles. Finally, your legs are pushed farther to the outside.

Subsequent to the exercise, slowly move your legs back together again.

D **28**: Forward Bend of the Upper Body in a Straddle Position

Stretching:
++ Inner thigh and back muscles

Starting Position

Sit on the floor with your legs stretched out to either side of your upright torso in a straddle position. Your training partner kneels behind you and puts his or her hands on your back. Your partner pushes you slowly to the front until you experience a minor stretch stimulus and you communicate this to him or her. For this exercise it is important that the push is applied to the lower back and not to the upper back.

Relaxing–Extending

Maintain the position and consciously relax the muscles. Continue to breathe regularly. Once the stretch tension decreases, after a few seconds, your partner pushes you farther forward until you feel a new stimulus.

Tensing–Relaxing–Extending

Tense your back against your partner's pushing hands. Your partner maintains his or her position so that the starting position remains intact. You then release the tension and briefly relax the tensed muscles. Finally, your partner pushes you farther forward toward the ground.

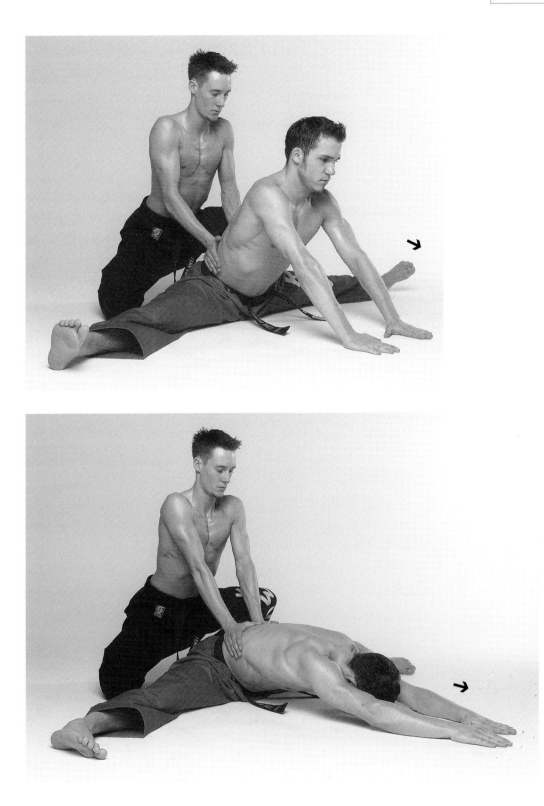

D 29: Outside Knee Push in a Supine Position

> Stretching:
> ++ Inner thigh muscles

Starting Position

Lie on your back with the legs bent, the soles of your feet resting on the ground, and the knees up. Your training partner kneels in front of you, his or her hands on your knees. Your partner slowly and carefully pushes your knees out and down on each side of your body until you feel a minor stretch stimulus and you communicate this to your partner.

Relaxing–Extending

Maintain the position and consciously relax the muscles. Continue to breathe regularly. Once the stretch tension decreases, after a few seconds, your partner pushes your knees farther down until you experience a new stimulus.

Tensing–Relaxing–Extending

Tense the inside of your knees against the hands of your partner, who does not retract, so that the starting position remains intact. You then release the tension and briefly relax the tensed muscles. Finally, your partner pushes your knees farther down.

Subsequently, move your knees closer together and slowly straighten the legs. Repeat the previous stretching method with straight legs.

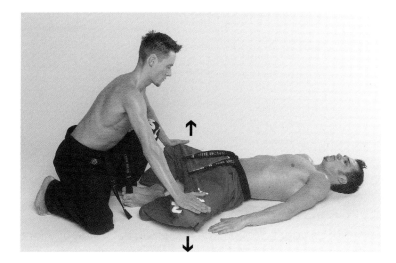

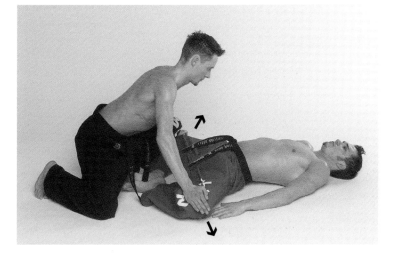

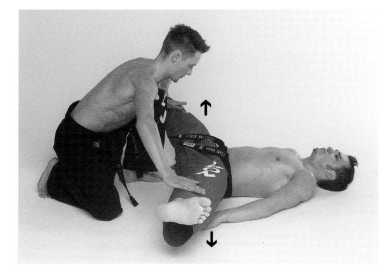

D 30: Pushing the Leg Up While Lying on the Back

> Stretching:
> ++ Rear thigh muscles
> + Calf muscles and gluteus muscles

Starting Position

Lie on your back with one leg straight and raised as high and back toward your body as possible. Your partner grips the leg and slowly and carefully pushes it farther toward your body. As soon as you experience a minor stretch stimulus, you communicate this to your partner, who stabilizes the position.

If your lower leg starts to lift up during the course of the exercise, your partner should push it back down.

Relaxing–Extending

Maintain the position and consciously relax the muscles. Continue to breathe regularly. Once the stretch tension decreases, after a few seconds, your partner pushes your leg farther until you experience a new stimulus.

Tensing–Relaxing–Extending

Tense the rear leg muscles against your partner, who maintains his or her stance so that the starting position remains intact. You then release the tension and briefly relax the tensed muscles. Finally, your leg is pushed up farther.

Part III: Stamina Training Exercises

CHAPTER **10**

Training Effects

Stamina training is an important component in the fitness training of martial arts athletes. Regular stamina training ensures your ability to endure the physical strain in martial arts for a longer period of time. In training and competition you remain concentrated and physically fit. In addition, you strengthen your immune system and sleep better, thereby accelerating the regeneration of your body.

Start the stamina training with moderate intensity. Initially you must build up your basic endurance before you start training sessions with intensive strain. Good basic endurance capabilities result in the lowering of the resting pulse rate and the exercising pulse rate. In addition, the pulse quickly returns to a normal rate, which is why physical activities are perceived to be less strenuous. The athlete remains fit for longer periods and experiences the sport session as less intensive. Many beginners in stamina training exercise at too high of an intensity. This poses an additional strain for the body and makes it susceptible to infections and injuries. Start your stamina training with moderate intensity and incrementally increase the demands.

Moderate stamina training produces many positive effects for your health and fitness in competitive sports.

Strengthening of the Heart Muscle

Regular stamina training exercises your heart muscle, which grows in size, and increases the volume of the heartbeat. Because of its higher performance capacity, less strain will be exerted, as it has to pump less in comparison with an untrained heart muscle. The resting pulse rate will be lower, the pulse rate will not increase as rapidly during exercise, and the pulse rate will return back to normal much quicker.

Stress Relief

Everyday stress has a negative impact on the body and attacks the immune system. Intensive training of any type, as well as martial arts competitions, also cause stress. Moderate stamina training enables the body to reduce the effects of stress. You feel and sleep better. After a few weeks of regular stamina training, you feel fit and ready to perform.

Stabilization of the Immune System

Regular low-intensity stimulation strengthens the immune system. To this end, your stamina training should be moderate. However, if your stamina training is done at a high exercising pulse rate, you subject your body to extra stress hormones and weaken the body's defenses.

Strengthening of the Locomotor System

Regular sports activities develop the muscles and the body's fitness. For this reason, stamina training also has a strengthening effect on the muscles of the locomotor system, though not as well focused on certain muscle groups as in power training. Against this backdrop, you should use varying types of stamina training, thereby strengthening different parts of the body. Cycling, for example, predominantly activates the leg muscles; swimming, in contrast, activates the muscles of the whole body.

CHAPTER 11

The Correct Training Intensity

The best possible training intensity depends on your physical shape and training aims. For beginners, basic stamina training is of particular importance. Advanced students should engage in regular basic stamina and fitness stamina sessions. This book differentiates among the following intensity areas.

1. Regenerative Training Area

This area comprises activities of very low intensity—for example, walking, slow cycling, and swimming. You will be in this area for as long as you perceive the exertion to be comfortable. However, you exceed the regenerative intensity once the exercise becomes strenuous. After a strenuous sports activity, a low level of intensity is recommended for a faster regeneration process. Immediately after training, you can jog for another 5–10 minutes. You can also plan a separate training session for this intensity area. For example, if you have trained intensively the previous day or have taken part in a competition, which left the body tired and the muscles tense, this type of training can accelerate the regeneration of your body.

2. Basic Stamina Area

From a health standpoint, this is the most important training. This degree of intensity improves the blood circulation and strengthens the immune system, and a substantial share of the energy used is extracted from the body's fat. You are in this area for as long as you are still able to speak while exercising. The intensity is too high if you feel tired and exhausted while exercising. The recommended types of sport are jogging, cycling, walking, and indoor training in connection with a cardio device. Well-trained basic stamina has a positive effect on all types of sport. The pulse rate quickly returns to normal, and the time required for regeneration is shorter than the regeneration time for fitness stamina training. This is of particular importance in competition, as this will make you fit and focused for longer periods. Regular training in this area lowers the resting pulse rate. After just a few weeks of basic stamina training, you will be able to perform better at the same pulse rate—for example, you can run longer distances and faster.

3. Fitness Stamina Area

In this area you develop the muscles and your general fitness. During the training process you feel strained with this grade of intensity, and after training the muscles feel clearly more strained as well. To this end, you can use any conceivable type of stamina training. Those in which the grade of intensity can be adapted to the required level of intensity are particularly recommended. This training intensity is the precondition for advanced athletes to achieve performance improvements. Before you start with this type of training, you must have initially built up a solid stamina base. Stamina training in the area of fitness can also be enjoyed more, as you do not exceed the intensity area even though you increase your running speed. In addition, if done correctly, the body regenerates quickly and fitness returns soon after training.

4. High-Intensity Area

In the threshold area between aerobic and anaerobic energy generation, the body is trained to withstand higher strain for longer periods. In the process, the body gains part of its energy anaerobically—that is, the body is unable to take in sufficient oxygen for energy conversion. The body now primarily "burns" carbohydrates, in the process of which the residuary substance lactate, the salt of lactic acid, is produced. The lactate cannot be broken down quickly by the body. Once the threshold between aerobic and anaerobic energy generation is exceeded—for example, during a hard exchange of blows in an infight—the production of lactic acid will increase disproportionately. This causes hyperacidity, and the activity must be stopped after a short time.

Health- and fitness-oriented stamina training is not aimed at training in this high-intensity area. However, some of professional athletes' training sessions are in the anaerobic area. This requires a solid stamina base, so that the pulse rate will quickly go down after the exertion, and training can continue.

✖ Hard pad training: the way to develop stamina in the high-intensity area.

Determination of the Optimum Training Intensity

You initially determine the maximum heart rate. On this basis you can then determine training areas.

MHR (maximum heart rate) = 220 minus your age. This method has been proved by many tests; however, it may be different for some individuals. Professional athletes frequently use the maximum heart rate test in which the pulse is pushed to the maximum by the intensity of training. This could include, for example, a sprint up to the personal performance limit. This is not recommended for fitness athletes, as the unusually intensive strain entails a high risk of injury.

Maximum heart rate (MHR)	220 minus your age
Regenerative training area	approximately 65% of the MHR
Basic stamina area	approximately 75% of the MHR
Fitness stamina area	approximately 85% of the MHR

Example:	Individual 40 years of age
Maximum heart rate, using simplified formula:	220 – 40 = 180 MHR
Regenerative training area:	180 x 0.65 = 117 HR
Basic stamina area:	180 x 0.75 = 135 HR
Fitness area:	180 x 0.85 = 153 HR

Your Training Area

In your training session try to come close to your optimum pulse rate.

Training pulse rate
Regenerative training area
Basic stamina area
Fitness stamina area

Measuring the Intensity

Measure your pulse rate by holding the wrist and placing your index and middle fingers on the inside of the arm above the joint of the thumb. Count the pulse beats for 20 seconds and multiply the result by 3 to determine beats per minute. Measure the resting pulse rate and the pulse rate after training. However, this method cannot be used during exercise, as you would have to interrupt the activity.

For stamina training you should use a pulse rate meter. This method requires a belt around the chest, which measures the heartbeats. A specialized wristwatch will show the results. These measuring devices can usually be adjusted in accordance with your individual pulse zone for training. Excessive values trigger an audible signal. Good models are available starting from approximately $100.

✖ Sparring and competition. A solid basic stamina lowers the pulse rate during the short breaks between the attacks. Thus, you save energy and remain fit for longer periods. However, fitness stamina must also be developed for staying power while sparring.

CHAPTER 12

Selection of a Stamina-Enhancing Type of Sport

Regular stamina training strengthens your heart and blood circulation and reduces the body fat. Significant advances in training can be achieved with little effort. Engage in stamina training regularly three times a week, with each training session lasting at least 40 minutes. In this way you will soon realize how the desired training targets can be achieved.

All types of sports are generally suited for your moderate stamina training, which is carried out with steady intensity. These include the classics of stamina training—jogging, cycling, and swimming—as well as jump rope and training in connection with cardio devices at fitness clubs. Select a sport in which you can maintain a steady speed throughout the training session, so that the pulse rate stays in the planned intensity zone. Martial arts training also includes stamina training. However, this is carried out with continuously changing intensity, which is why it is sensible to engage in additional stamina training sessions in the areas of basic stamina and fitness stamina.

Once you have achieved a solid stamina base, you can add interval training to the stamina training. For example, carry out fast sprints when jogging and running, and, subsequently, reduce your speed again. Your body gets used to exertion of different intensities and learns to quickly regulate the pulse rate after the exertion.

Jogging

More and more people have discovered jogging as a means of gaining fitness and relief at the end of a stressful day. Jogging is a natural type of movement that can be carried out nearly everywhere. You can jog when and where you like. Opportunities to carry out this type of sport can be found in a large number of places—for example, in a park or forest. Running is something you learned as a child. Therefore, you can promptly start with the training. In contrast, other types of sport, such as swimming and cross-country skiing, require a learning process for their special techniques. Jogging does not necessitate special expenditures: shorts, a T-shirt, and a pair of running shoes suffice.

Although jogging does not require learning a special technique, the more peaceful and relaxed your jogging is, the more comfortable and energy saving the training will be. Therefore, it is worthwhile to pay attention to your style from time to time and, if required, to make minor changes. Do not attempt to change your jogging technique by force, or you will tense up during jogging. There are top athletes whose running style does not correspond to the ideal picture of a running athlete.

Optimum Style

When jogging, keep your upper body erect and look several yards ahead. Jog with steady steps of medium length and move the hip forward with each step. Your foot returns to the ground with the heel first, after which you roll across the entire foot and start your next step.

The arms are roughly at a 90-degree angle and easily swing along during the run. The hands are loosely closed as fists, and the thumb rests on the index finger. Always ensure that the shoulder, neck, and face muscles remain relaxed.

Training

You should warm up prior to jogging. Walk at a moderate speed for a few minutes, then perform stretching exercises. To avoid injuries, you must at least stretch the muscle groups that are used for jogging. These are, in particular, the calf muscles and the muscles of the front and rear thighs. You should never skip the warm-up and the preparatory stretching exercises. In this way you prepare the body for training, fitness will increase, and muscle tensions will be loosened.

At the end of training, continue to jog or walk at a moderate speed for a few minutes and stretch the activated muscles. This accelerates the regeneration process and the reduction of lactate, as well as prevents the shortening of your muscles.

Cycling

Cycling strengthens the leg muscles, particularly the muscles of the front thigh. The training intensity in cycling can be controlled better than in jogging because the complete weight of the body must be moved during jogging, whereas in cycling the body is supported by the saddle. Thus, fewer muscle groups are strained and the joints are saved. This type of training is particularly suited for fitness beginners and is also frequently used for rehabilitation—for example, following knee and foot injuries. However, it is also sensible for advanced athletes, as fast and powerful cycling can achieve a high pulse rate.

In cycling you should try to maintain an erect upper body, not bending forward when tired. Place the toes and the balls of the feet on the pedals. Adjust the saddle height so that the pushing leg still forms a slight angle at the lowest point of the pedal. If the leg is fully straightened, too much strain will be exerted on the knee joint.

Training

The warm-up for cycle training should include a few minutes of cycling at moderate speed and stretching exercises, particularly for the calf muscles and the muscles of the thigh. However, it is best to stretch all muscle groups, so that you do not feel any tension in the neck or back, for example.

It is better to cycle at a higher number of revolutions, than with great effort. Advanced athletes can intensify their cycle training by consecutive fast and slow intervals. You should also vary your cycle training. Alternate between different courses and vary the intensity. An hour on a stationary bicycle at the fitness club adds new demands to the program.

At the end of the training session you should continue with some easy cycling for a few minutes before you conclude the cycle training with stretching exercises for the activated muscles.

Swimming

Swimming molds the body and conditions the cardiovascular system. This type of training is particularly gentle to the joints, as the water carries the weight of the body. Changes in the speed of swimming make it possible to achieve the desired exertion.

Three swimming styles are specifically recommended for stamina training, as these can be trained with similar intensity over a longer period of time: breaststroke, crawl, and backstroke. Alternate between these styles to strengthen a variety of muscles.

Training

Prior to the training there should be a warm-up phase. Swim a few lengths of the pool at a slow speed to warm up, then carry out some stretching exercises at the side.

In the main phase of the training, swim for a minimum of 20 minutes. Advanced athletes can extend the time significantly and vary the training speed—for example, by swimming one length at high speed, two lengths for regeneration, and then increasing the speed again.

Conclude the training with some very easy swimming and stretching of the activated muscles.

Jump Rope

Jump rope is an important type of training for all martial arts, as it develops stamina, power, coordination, and speed. For example, you will quickly realize how your coordination abilities improve. After just a few training sessions, you will be able to perform many more skips without getting tangled in the rope.

The Correct Length of Rope

Hold one end of the rope in each hand and place both feet on the middle of the rope. Extend the arms sideways at about a 45-degree angle to the ribs. That is the correct rope length for jump rope. Shorten the rope until the handles are in the required position. If you use a jump rope without handles, wrap the ends of the rope around your hands to achieve the optimum length.

Training

To warm up, skip easily and relaxed for one round. To avoid injury, do not perform any high jumps or complicated skips. Subsequently, stretch at least those muscle groups that are primarily used in jump rope.

The main part of jump rope depends on the progress made in your training. For beginners it is recommended to skip for three 2-minute rounds, with a 1-minute break between each round. Include more and more skips in the program as you progress in your training sessions. Advanced athletes can increase the rounds to five 3-minute rounds. They can also include intervals—for example, the fastest possible skips in the last 30 seconds of a round. Skilled athletes skip without a break for a minimum of 20 minutes and perform various jumps at different speeds. The training concludes with slow and simple skips, thus lowering the pulse rate, followed by stretching the activated muscles once again.

✖ The running skip.

Skips

Try to skip with little effort, an erect upper body, and relaxed shoulders. Commence your jump across the toes and the balls of your feet, then return to this starting position.

1. Standard Jump

Swing the rope from back to front over your head. Jump simultaneously with both feet above the swinging rope and return to the floor with both feet at the same time. Return smoothly to the balls of the feet.

2. Running Skip

Skip as if you were running. Jump with one foot across the swinging rope then jump onto the other foot. This is the fastest possible skipping technique.

3. One-Leg Skip

Skip several times with one foot across the swinging rope before you change the skipping leg. Beginners will clearly feel the intensity after five skips. Advanced athletes can easily perform 20 consecutive skips on the same leg.

4. Skipping with Bent Knees

Pull one knee toward your upper body while you jump across the rope with the other leg. Then pull up the skipping leg and jump with the other leg. Alternate between the right and left leg and continue to pull up the knee of the other leg.

5. Skipping with Crossed Arms

Skilled athletes succeed with this type of skip. This way they demonstrate their fitness and particularly their coordination abilities. Jump off the floor and cross the arms in front of your body before the rope passes through below the feet. Open the cross as soon as the rope is above the body.

6. Skipping with Double Rotation

Jump with both feet high above the ground and pull your knees toward the upper body. In the process, skip the rope twice before your feet return to the floor. Due to the necessary jumping power and high coordination requirements, only advanced athletes can perform this skip.

Part IV: Power Training Exercises

CHAPTER **13**

Basics

Power training will improve your performance in martial arts. Regular power training by balanced exercising of all the body's muscle groups is recommended (see pp. 10–17). Additional strength improves your power in punching, pushing, and kicking. In addition, strong muscles enable you to better withstand the opponent's blows. Muay Thai professionals from Thailand, for example, are known for their extraordinary ability to withstand blows. This is the result of intensive strengthening of their neck muscles. Blocking an opponent's techniques is easier with strong muscles. In martial arts, some muscle groups are exerted more than others, which makes the athlete susceptible to injuries. Regular power training can prevent the development of such muscle imbalance.

In this chapter you will learn the most effective exercises for power training. Exercises have been selected that are particularly suitable for martial arts athletes and by which all muscle groups can be strengthened in a balanced way. Exercises are included for all muscle groups and can be carried out with inexpensive small accessories for use in your training at home.

What Is Muscle Power?

Muscle power is the ability to overcome a resistance (for example, to lift a weight), to counteract it (for example, to lower a weight in a controlled manner), or to hold on to it (for example, to maintain a weight in a certain position). The three types of muscle power are maximum power, stamina power, and resilience.

The *maximum power* is the highest possible power that the muscles can generate (for example, to lift a dumbbell). It depends on the available power potential and the ability to apply this power potential.

Stamina power is the ability to use the power as frequently as possible in a certain period of time (for example, repeated lifting of a dumbbell), or to maintain the power performance over an extended time period (for example, keeping a dumbbell in a certain position).

Resilience is the ability to carry out a power performance as quickly as possible (for example, the fastest possible lifting of a dumbbell). To this end, the muscles contributing to the move must contract.

Muscle Reaction to Training Stimuli

The muscles' adaptability to the power training depends on which training methods you use (see pp. 111–115).

Greater Power Potential (Maximum Power–Muscle Size)

The maximum power depends on the power potential and the ability to apply the power potential. The muscle size represents the power potential. Training stimuli in power training result in muscle growth (hypertrophy).

The muscle development method provides the best possible training results in terms of muscle growth.

Improved Activation Ability (Maximum Power–Muscle Power)

It is impossible to use the full power potential to overcome a resistance. However, you are in a position to improve muscle coordination (intermuscular coordination) and to hone your capabilities in activating the greatest number of muscle tendons to overcome a resistance (intramuscular coordination). In this way you will succeed in making better use of your power potential.

Training with the maximum power method clearly improves the activation capability of your muscles.

Quicker Contraction Capability (Resilience)

You will improve your takeoff power by training your muscles so that they quickly contract during a move.

Optimum results are achieved by the power resilience method. Maximum power training also has a positive effect on resilience.

Extended Power of Resistance (Stamina Power)

You will develop your stamina by concentrating your training on the maintenance of power performance.

Training with the stamina power method achieves the best results. Maximum power training also increases stamina power.

CHAPTER 14

Training Methods

Martial arts athletes concentrate their training mainly on the stamina power method or the muscle development method. The primary aims of stamina power training are a slender body and good stamina, whereas the muscle development method is aimed at the development of a muscular body and the strengthening of muscle power. Untrained athletes must initially improve their stamina power before they start to develop their muscle power.

To further improve their performance capabilities, advanced athletes should also carry out exercises aimed at the development of their maximum power and resilience.

1. Stamina Power Method

Users:	Beginners, advanced and competitive athletes
Repetitions:	15–30
Speed:	Slow to swift
Intensity per set (subjective):	Medium to hard
Break between two sets:	1–2 minutes
Use:	As a separate session or after the resilience or maximum power method
Training targets:	Stamina improvement, reduction of body fat

Choose the degree of difficulty of the exercise so that you can repeat it 15–30 times in one set. The speed can be slow to swift; regular breathing is important. At the end of the set, you should feel moderately to very exhausted.

Rest 1–2 minutes between sets. As a variant, advanced athletes can promptly add a training set for the opposite muscles—for example, alternate between training the front and rear upper arm muscles. This training provides sufficient time for the regeneration of the initially trained muscle, which can, subsequently, be exercised again.

The stamina power method can be scheduled as a separate training session. Or you can initially carry out some exercises in accordance with the resilience or maximum power method followed by exercises in accordance with the stamina power method.

The main objectives of the method are the improvement of your stamina and the creation of a slender and strong body. This is why the method is used by athletes who usually have problems in reaching their weight limits.

2. Muscle Development Method

Users:	Beginners, advanced and competitive athletes
Repetitions:	8–12
Speed:	Slow
Intensity per set (subjective):	Hard to very hard
Break between two sets:	2–3 minutes
Use:	As a separate session or after the resilience or maximum power method
Training targets:	Muscle development, increase in maximum power

Choose the degree of difficulty of the exercise so that you can repeat it 8–12 times in one set. The moves should be rather slow. At the end, you should feel very exhausted but still be able to avoid wrong positioning and incorrect movements.

Take a break of 2–3 minutes between sets. As a variant you can promptly exercise the opposite muscles for one set.

The method can be scheduled as a separate training session. Or you can initially carry out some exercises in accordance with the resilience or maximum power method followed by exercises in accordance with the muscle development method.

The main objectives of this method are the development of muscle mass and an increase in maximum power.

3. Resilience Method

Users:	Competitive athletes
Repetitions:	6–12
Speed:	Explosive
Intensity per set (subjective):	Hard to very hard
Break between two sets:	2–3 minutes
Use:	After warm-up phase and warm-up sets
Training targets:	Fast release of power in martial arts techniques

Choose the degree of difficulty so that you can repeat it 6–12 times in one set. Carry out explosive moves. At the end you should feel exhausted to very exhausted. Take a 2–3 minute break between two sets.

The method is carried out at the beginning of a training session in accordance with the warm-up phase and 1–2 warm-up sets. The body must be rested; otherwise, it will be very prone to injuries. Complex basic exercises such as K 1: Bench Press and K 31: Squat are usually used in this method. Subsequently, the remaining exercises of the training session should involve the muscle development or stamina power method.

The resilience method is only suitable for very advanced athletes. It is used for more explosive martial arts techniques in competition.

4. Maximum Power Method

Users:	Competitive athletes
Repetitions:	1–3
Speed:	Swift
Intensity per set (subjective):	Very hard
Break between two sets:	3–5 minutes
Use:	After warm-up phase and warm-up sets
Training targets:	Greater release of power in martial arts techniques

Choose the degree of difficulty so that you can repeat it 1–3 times in one set. The moves should be carried out swiftly. At the end, you should feel very much exhausted. Take a break of 3–5 minutes between sets.

The method is carried out at the beginning of a training session after a warm-up phase and some warm-up sets. The body must be rested; otherwise, it will be very susceptible to injuries. The method usually contains some basic exercises, such as K 31: Squat. Subsequently, the remaining exercises of the training session are carried out in accordance with the stamina power method.

The maximum power method is only suitable for very advanced athletes. It is used for a greater release of power in competitive martial arts techniques—for example, to increase the power for a knockout.

Intensifying Techniques

You can increase the demand on your muscles in stamina power and muscle development training by the intensifying techniques no. 1 and 2 described on page 117.

Advanced athletes can also use the intensifying techniques no. 3–6 in muscle development training. However, these are too intensive for beginning athletes. The aim of muscle development training is the maximum exhaustion of the muscles, as the muscle-growth stimulus

✖ K 19: Concentration Curl.

develops in line with the degree of exhaustion. The intensifying techniques no. 3–6 result in greater exhaustion of the muscles, as they are exercised beyond the point of muscle failure. Initially, repeat an exercise 8–12 times up to the point of momentary muscle failure. Subsequently, use one of the intensifying techniques to achieve even greater muscle exhaustion.

When using intensifying techniques, extend the length of the regeneration phase.

1. Maintaining the End Position

The exercises are intensified if you remain in the end position for about 3 seconds before repeating the exercise. Simultaneously, the muscles are tensed at maximum strength. Do not hold your breath, but continue to breathe at regular intervals.

2. Partial Moves in the End Position

Partial moves are a sensible variant to the increase in muscle activity. This means minor and slow moves up and down in the end position. Repetitions in the area of highest muscle activity improve the training results. Always ensure regular breathing.

3. Partial Repeats

Exercise with a complete movement radius up to the point of momentary muscle failure. Then continue without interruption with a few repetitions of the exercise, but with a reduced radius of movement. For example, in K 20: Standing Biceps Curl, raise the barbell slightly a few more times after the momentary muscle failure.

4. Intensifying Repeats

Exercise up to the point of momentary muscle failure. Then continue without interruption with some supported repeats in the course of the exertion phase. As soon as you are unable to control your weight when returning to the starting position, stop the exercise. In the exercise K 1: Bench Press, for example, your training partner supports you in lifting the weight. However, lowering must be carried out on your own. In the exercise K 19: Concentration Curl, you support the lifting of the weight with your free hand.

5. Extended Sets

Train up to the point of momentary muscle failure, then lower the weight. Take a break of about 30 seconds and lift the weight again. Then carry out approximately 2–4 repetitions.

6. Combined Sets

Train up to the point of momentary muscle failure. Then promptly start another exercise for the same muscle group. The technique is based on the knowledge that different muscle tendons will be exhausted after the first and second exercise. For the upper arm muscles, for example, initially carry out the exercise K 19: Concentration Curl, followed by K 20: Standing Biceps Curl.

CHAPTER 15

Training Structure

One Set versus Several-Set Training

One "set" indicates the execution of one exercise from the first to the last repetition. Many different recommendations exist as to the number of sets that should be carried out in one training session. Basically, beginners will achieve muscle growth with just one set per exercise. Several sets per exercise will result in some additional muscle growth; however, this requires more time and it also increases the risk of overloading the body. A reasonable approach for beginners is to start with a program aimed at the complete body, which involves 1–2 sets per exercise, depending on the number of exercises.

Advanced and competitive athletes' training includes a great variety of programs and sets, with 2–5 intensive sets for each exercise recommended. It has been determined that successful training in this area can also be possible with only one set, assuming that the muscles are totally exhausted by the intensifying techniques. To avoid the risk of injury, the athlete must perform 1–2 warm-up sets with light weight prior to each exercise. After one exercise, athletes frequently carry out further exercises for the same muscle group.

The number of sets also depends on the total number of exercises in one training session. Intensive training in the main training phase should not exceed 60–90 minutes (see pp. 193–197).

Selection of a Training Weight/Intensity

As a beginner, carry out your exercises with light weight. Ask a fitness trainer for the initial weight or carefully approach the suitable weight. To this end, choose a light weight and carry out a few repetitions. If you feel a light strain to your muscles, but no pain and exertion, this weight should be kept as the starting weight in your training plan. You can increase the weight slightly in the following training sessions. However, you must always select the weight for each exercise so that you can carry out a minimum of 15 technically correct repetitions of the exercise. Increase the repetitions as you advance with your training. At the very latest, increase the weight once you have reached 30 repetitions. Choose the new training weight so that you can achieve a minimum of 15 repetitions. Continue to incrementally increase the repetitions in the following training sessions.

Advanced students significantly increase the weights in the process of training. Depending on the training method, choose the weights in such a way that you can carry out 15–30 repetitions (stamina power method) or 8–12 repetitions (muscle development method). Proceed with training in line with the aforementioned stamina power method. For the muscle development method, increase the weight after 12 repetitions, but only to the degree that you can achieve a minimum of 8 repetitions.

Training Frequency and Training Breaks

The greatest possible increase in performance according to the principle of super compensation will be achieved if the optimum relationship between exertion and regeneration time has been chosen (see pp. 6–9). How often a muscle group must be exercised and how long the subsequent break should be depend on many factors, such as the stimulus intensity, the progress in training, and the arrangement of regenerative measures. Therefore, the following are general guidelines only.

It generally applies that exercising a muscle group once a week serves to maintain strength; two to three times a week generates additional strength. If you adopt a program for the entire body, two to three sessions per week will suffice for progress; however, split training—that is, training sessions for different muscle groups—requires several sessions. Beginners with very little muscle mass can be successful with just one training session per week. This applies to competitive athletes and bodybuilders as well, who can also achieve significant muscle growth if they very intensively train one muscle group once a week. To this end, the muscle groups are allocated to several training sessions, in which each muscle group is trained to maximum exhaustion in several exercises, sets, and intensifying techniques.

Training with the stamina power method requires a minimum of one day for regeneration of the activated muscle groups. Beginners must take a break for two days if they perceive the exertion as medium to hard. Training in accordance with the muscle development method requires a regeneration period of one to three days, the exact time period depending on the training intensity and the regeneration measures. For example, an athlete can carry out easy stamina training and stretching exercises the following day, which even cuts the time needed for regeneration. Intensive resilience or maximum power training require an even longer break in training.

Training programs for martial arts athletes must take into account that the muscles are not activated intensively only in power training

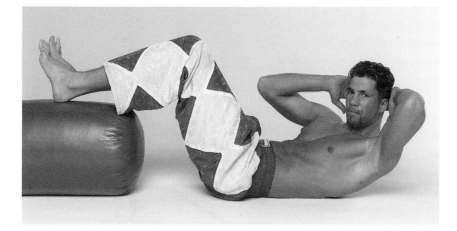

but also in martial arts training. If the athlete, for example, carries out a training session with intensifying techniques for the chest muscles, it is not advisable to conduct boxing training the following day. The athlete would be more susceptible to injuries, as the muscles are tired; in addition, they are unable to offer a full performance potential.

Exercise Sequence in Strengthening

The strengthening exercises described in Chapters 16 and 17 are organized by muscle group. Start your training with one large muscle group, such as the chest or thigh muscles. Carry out complex exercises initially, before you begin with the isolated strengthening of a muscle group, to prevent its exhaustion. Otherwise, wrong positioning and incorrect compensatory movements could lead to injuries. For this reason, the muscles of the upper arm are exercised at the end of the upper body exercises and, likewise, the calf muscles at the end of the leg exercises. Another training principle includes an initial isolated exercise to prevent early tiring. However, this principle should be used only by very advanced power athletes.

The strengthening of the abdominal and lower back muscles should occur only at the end of training. If you start with intensive training of these muscle groups, it will be difficult to stabilize your upper body during the subsequent complex exercises.

Rules

Take a stable starting position, so that you can fully concentrate on the execution of your exercise. Tense your abdominal muscles for stabilization of the upper body, and keep the back straight. Exercises in a standing position will also tense the muscles of your buttocks. Prior to exercises with dumbbells always check the fastening, particularly prior to moves above your head.

Perform the exercise with regular, rather slow moves and pay attention to a technically correct execution. The aim of power training is the effective training of the muscles, not the lifting of maximum weight. Concentrate in each exercise on the target muscles and consciously experience how they work during training. Avoid working up momentum or making incorrect compensatory movements using other muscle groups. For example, during K 20: Standing Biceps Curl, you will find out how the front muscles of the upper arm shake and tire. Through rapid moves, shoulder rotation, and raising of the neck, you may possibly succeed in lifting the barbell one more time. However, this does not result in better conditioning of the upper arm because the additional repetition only occurs by taking the wrong position and using other muscle groups.

The muscles to be trained must be kept tensed during the complete exercise. In the course of the biceps curl, for example, you must not drop the lower arm to a fully straight position, but keep the muscles of the upper arm tensed. The muscle activity increases during dumbbell lifting and is at its most intense in the end position. This is why maintaining the end position and making partial moves can also intensify the exercise.

Regularly control the starting position and the exercise execution by practicing in front of a mirror. Ensure that the shoulders remain at the same level. Bending the wrists during an exercise increases the risk of tendinitis.

Maintain regular breathing during exercises with light weights and low intensity, and during those carried out slowly or statically. If you interrupt the rhythm of your breath, your body will receive insufficient

✖ K 20: Standing Biceps Curl.

oxygen, which poses a considerable health risk. If you carry out exercises with heavy weights, high intensity, and high speed, inhale prior to each move, exhale during the exertion, and inhale again when you return to the starting position. Maintain this rhythm during all repetitions. If the end position is maintained for a few seconds for intensification, continue to breathe regularly.

You may strain and exhaust yourself during the exercises. During stamina power training you can have many repetitions, and you can move heavy weights during muscle development training. However, once you experience pain, the exercise must be interrupted. If the pain decreases during the rest break, consider the reason for the pain—for example, a wrong body stance—and try again. If the same pain reappears, stop the exercise and continue with the next one in your training plan. Should the pain not disappear during the rest break, stop your training and consult a physician.

Always perform your exercises for the left and right side of your body with the same intensity, for balanced training of your body. All important muscle groups must be included in the training program.

You can change the shape of your body only by regular exercise. Beginners should train at least twice per week, advanced athletes more often. If you pause for longer periods, your muscle strength and size will slowly decrease. Try to maintain your schedule of once-a-week training even though you may have little time to spare.

However, if you are sick, you must abstain from training, as training may jeopardize the healing process.

Beginners should carry out the exercises with little strain. It is better to choose weights/intensities that are too low rather than too high. Muscles get used to new demands quicker than do the tendons and cords, which is why the body must be accustomed slowly to an intensification of exercises. First increase the number of repetitions and sets, before you increase the weights/intensities. If the demands increase too rapidly, the body will be in danger of being hurt.

CHAPTER 16

Strengthening Exercises for the Upper Body

This chapter introduces you to the best exercises for the upper body, as contained in the power training of martial arts athletes. You will learn about exercises with dumbbells and barbells, bodyweight exercises, as well as exercises on machines. This will enable you to develop all of the body's muscle groups effectively, regardless of whether your training takes place at home or at a fitness club. If a training device is not available, use a different exercise that activates the same muscle group.

Some muscle groups on the following pages have been combined for better clarity. More detailed information about the muscle functions can be found on pages 10–17.

Execution of the Exercises

Take the starting position and perform the exercise in accordance with the exercise description. Repeat the execution for as often as is required by the training method you use (see pp. 111–115). You must select a weight that permits technically correct repetitions—without wrong positioning or incorrect compensatory movements (see pp. 122–124). Advanced athletes can use intensifying techniques (see pp. 116–118). Although an exercise is described for only one side, it should be done on both sides, as both sides of the body must always be strengthened together.

The description of the exercises indicates whether the strengthening is of primary (++) or secondary (+) importance for the muscles.

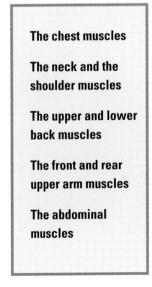

The chest muscles

The neck and the shoulder muscles

The upper and lower back muscles

The front and rear upper arm muscles

The abdominal muscles

The Chest Muscles

K 1: Bench Press

> **Strengthening:**
> **++ Chest muscles**
>   **+ Front shoulder and rear upper arm muscles**

Starting Position

Lie on your back on a weight bench. The arms point vertically upward, little more than shoulder-width apart. In your hands, hold dumbbells, with the thumbs pointing toward each other. Tense your abdominal muscles to avoid a hollow back.

Execution

Lower the dumbbells and move them slightly sideways until the upper arms are nearly horizontal. Then push the dumbbells back into the starting position. Ensure that the wrists and the back are kept straight, and avoid making incorrect compensatory movements with the shoulders.

Variant

If the weight bench has a weight rest, you can train with a barbell and heavy weights.

If the weight bench has an adjustable back, use it to strengthen different parts of the chest muscles.

K **2**: Flies Lying on the Back

> **Strengthening:**
> ++ Chest muscles
> + Front shoulder muscles

Starting Position

Lie on your back either on the floor or on a weight bench. The arms point vertically upward. Hold dumbbells, with the palms of the hands facing each other. The abdominal muscles are tight and the wrists are straight.

Execution

Move the slightly bent arms to the outside, so that they are nearly horizontal, but do not rest them on the ground. Briefly maintain this position before you slowly return the arms to the starting position. Pay attention to slow and regular moves and avoid a hollow back or extending the arms too far backward.

Variant

If you have a weight bench, you can lower the upper arms to the horizontal position, which increases the intensity of the exercise.

K 3: Push-up

> **Strengthening:**
> ++ Chest muscles
> + Front shoulder and rear upper arm muscles

Starting Position

Go down to the floor face down and support your weight with the hands and toes. The hands are shoulder-width apart with the fingers pointing forward. Tighten the abdominal muscles and the muscles of the buttocks for stabilization of the back. Look down.

Execution

Bend your arms until the upper body nearly touches the floor, but do not rest on the ground. Then straighten the arms and return to your starting position. Pay attention to having a straight back during the exercise.

Variant

Changes in the positioning of your hands will have an effect on different parts of the chest muscles. Well-trained athletes can place their toes on an object, thereby intensifying the exercise.

For training of your takeoff power, you can push off the ground from the lower position and clap your hands.

K 4: Chest Press on a Machine

> **Strengthening:**
> ++ Chest muscles
>   + Front shoulder and rear upper arm muscles

Starting Position

Adjust the device in accordance with your body size. The handles must be somewhat below your shoulders, and your back must fully rest against the cushion. Tense the abdominal muscles for stabilization of your position.

Execution

Push the handles forward in a regular movement, so that the arms are nearly straight. Then slowly return to the starting position. Pay attention to straight wrists and do not retract the elbows too far behind the upper body, so as to avoid excess strain to the shoulder joints.

Variant

The majority of equipment offers horizontal and vertical handle positions. Change the handles after a few training sessions to strengthen different parts of the chest muscles.

K 5: Flies on a Machine

Strengthening:
++ Chest muscles
 + Front shoulder muscles

Starting Position

Adjust the equipment in accordance with your body size. The handles must be somewhat below your shoulders. Use the equipment's support, if available, to take hold of the handles. The upper arms are now extended in line with the shoulders, and the back is fully resting against the rear cushion. Tense the abdominal muscles.

Execution

Move the lever arms in a simultaneous motion toward each other, so that they nearly touch. Then slowly return to the starting position, but not beyond it, to avoid excess strain to the shoulder joints. Pay attention to straight wrists and avoid raising or making other incorrect compensatory movements with the shoulders.

The Neck Muscles and the Shoulder Muscles

K 6: Overhead Press

> **Strengthening:**
> ++ Shoulder muscles, particularly the lateral part
> + Neck and rear upper arm muscles

Starting Position

Sit erect on a chair. The bent arms are up in the air. The elbows point to the outside, so that your head is between the dumbbells. Hold dumbbells with the thumbs pointing toward each other. Tighten the abdominal muscles.

Execution

Raise both dumbbells at the same time without changing the position of your hands on the dumbbells. Keep your back straight. Then return your arms slowly to the starting position. Avoid moving the head forward or allowing the dumbbells to move to the front or rear.

Variant

You can also lift the dumbbells from a frontal position. This will intensify the training of the front part of the shoulder muscles; however, it will reduce the effect on the lateral part of the shoulder muscles.

K **7**: Lateral Raises

> **Strengthening:**
> **++ Shoulder muscles, particularly the lateral part**
> **+ Neck muscles**

Starting Position

Stand upright with the legs slightly bent and the feet hip-width apart. The slightly bent arms are at the sides of your body or in front of the thighs. Hold dumbbells with the backs of your hands facing outward. Tense the abdominal muscles and the muscles of the buttocks and keep your wrists straight.

Execution

Raise the slightly bent arms sideways up to shoulder-height. This should not be a swinging motion. Ensure that the back remains straight and erect. Then slowly return the arms to the starting position. Avoid compensatory upward movements with the shoulders or the neck muscles.

Variant

Beginners can also do this exercise sitting down. Keep your arms at the sides of the body at a 90-degree angle and raised to a horizontal position.

You can carry out front-lifting, intensifying the training on the front part of the shoulder muscles. To do this, lift the dumbbells in front of the thighs with the thumbs pointing toward each other. Slowly raise the dumbbells to a horizontal position.

K **8**: Reverse Flies

> **Strengthening:**
> **++ Rear shoulder muscles**
> **+ Neck, lower and upper back, and lateral shoulder muscles**

Starting Position

From an upright stance, slightly bend the knees while shifting the buttocks to the back and the upper body to the front. Hold dumbbells, with the palms of the hands facing each other and your arms slightly bent. Tighten the abdominal muscles and the muscles of the buttocks and keep your back straight.

Execution

Raise the slightly bent arms until the upper arms are in line with the shoulders. At the end of the move, pull the shoulder blades together. Do not use a swinging motion, and ensure that the abdominal muscles remain tight. Then slowly return the dumbbells to the starting position. Avoid compensatory upward movements with the shoulder or neck muscles.

Variant

The exercise can also be carried out leaning forward in a sitting position, or in a prone position on a weight bench.

K 9: Shoulder Lifts

> **Strengthening:**
> ++ Neck muscles
> + Shoulder muscles

Starting Position

Stand upright with the legs slightly bent and hip-width apart. The arms are to the sides of your body and you are holding dumbbells. Tighten the abdominal muscles and the muscles of your buttocks.

Execution

Raise the shoulders as far as possible, the movement being generated entirely by the shoulders. Avoid lifting the weight upward by bending the arms. Then slowly lower the dumbbells and return to the starting position.

Variant

Intensify the exercise with a rear circular rotation of the shoulders. In the process, you should pay attention to regular breathing.

K 10: Reverse Flies on a Machine

> **Strengthening:**
> ++ Rear shoulder and neck muscles
>   + Lateral shoulder and lower and upper back muscles

Starting Position

Sit down facing the machine and take hold of the handles. Adjust the height of the seat so that the legs nearly form a right angle. Push your upper body against the cushion and tighten the abdominal muscles.

Execution

Move the handles together in a smooth motion to the back. At the end of the move, pull the shoulder blades together. Then slowly return the arms to the starting position. Keep the abdominal muscles tight, keep the wrists straight, and avoid raising the shoulders and the neck.

Variant

Some types of equipment have lower arm cushions instead of the handles. In that case, move the arms toward the rear in a U-shape.

The Upper and Lower Back Muscles

K 11: One-Armed Dumbbell Row

> **Strengthening:**
> ++ Upper back muscles
> + Front upper arm, neck, and rear shoulder muscles

Starting Position

Take a lunge step and support your weight with one hand on the front thigh. The arm on the other side is lowered. In the lowered hand, hold a dumbbell, with the palm of the hand facing the body. The back is straight, and the abdominal muscles and the muscles of the buttocks are tight.

Execution

Pull the elbow back and up as far as possible to the rear, keeping the elbow close to the body. Then slowly lower the arm, but do not completely straighten it. Avoid raising the shoulder throughout the exercise, and pay attention to keeping your upper body straight.

Variant

For better support, you can place the front hand on a chair or other object.

K **12**: Dumbbell Row with Both Arms

Strengthening:
++ Upper back muscles
+ Front upper arm, rear shoulder, neck, and lower back muscles

Starting Position

From an upright stance, slightly bend the knees while shifting the buttocks to the back and the upper body to the front. Hold dumbbells, with the palms of the hands facing each other. Tighten the abdominal muscles and the muscles of the buttocks and maintain a straight back.

Execution

Pull the elbows backward and upward and, at the end of the move, pull the shoulder blades together. The back is not moved in the process. Ensure that the abdominal muscles stay tight.

Variant

The closer you move the elbows along the ribs, the more the upper back muscles will be tensed. Accordingly, the exercise will be less intensive for the rear shoulder and the neck muscles.

   You can also exercise with a barbell, taking hold of it at shoulder-width.

K 13: Lateral Pulldown

> **Strengthening:**
> ++ **Upper back muscles**
> + **Upper chest, front upper arm, and rear shoulder muscles**

Starting Position

Sit down facing the equipment and take hold of the handle. Adjust the seat height so that the thigh and lower leg almost form a right angle. Place the feet firmly on the ground, and tighten the abdominal muscles for stabilization of the position.

Execution

Pull the handle in a smooth movement down to your neck while lowering your elbows toward the ribs. Then slowly return the arms to the starting position. Avoid raising the shoulders and the neck, and keep the abdominal muscles tense to avoid a hollow back.

Variant

You can also pull the handle toward the chest, with the upper body leaning somewhat to the rear but with a straight back. This variant intensifies the effect on the chest muscles.

K 14: Chin-up

Strengthening:
++ Upper back muscles
 + Shoulder and front upper arm muscles

Starting Position

Hang freely on a chin-up bar. The arms are shoulder-width apart or slightly wider, while the palms of the hands point to the front. The body is straight and the abdominal muscles are tight.

Execution

Pull yourself up in a smooth motion while moving the elbows toward the ribs. Briefly maintain the position before you slowly return to the starting position. Lower the body only insofar that the arms remain slightly bent, keeping the tension in the muscles. Avoid making compensatory movements such as raising the shoulders.

Variant

Beginners can use the floor or a chair for support, so that they do not have to lift their entire weight.

You can also take a closer grip on the bar with the back of your hands pointing forward, a palm's width apart. This will be more intensive training for the front upper arm and the front shoulder muscles.

K **15**: Leaning the Upper Body Forward

> **Strengthening:**
> **++ Lower back muscles**
> **+ Upper back, neck, rear shoulder, thigh, and gluteus muscles**

Starting Position

Standing with your back straight, lean your upper body forward slightly with the knees somewhat bent and the legs shoulder-width apart. With the palms of the hands facing toward you, hold dumbbells in front of the thighs. Tighten the muscles of the buttocks and the abdominal muscles for stabilization of the position.

Execution

Lower the upper body to the front while pushing the buttocks to the rear. Pay attention to a straight back. Briefly maintain the position before returning to the starting position. Pay particular attention to tight abdominal muscles.

Variant

Beginners must initially learn the exercise without additional weight, as an incorrect execution of this exercise entails a high risk of injury.

Advanced athletes can bend their upper body to a horizontal position.

K 16: Raising the Body from a Prone Position

> **Strengthening:**
> ++ **Lower back muscles**
> + **Neck, rear shoulder, and rear thigh muscles**

Starting Position

Lie on the floor in a prone position, the arms extended forward on the floor and the forehead on the floor. Tighten the abdominal muscles and the muscles of the buttocks. To avoid a hollow back, you can put a towel underneath your stomach.

Execution

Raise the head, left arm, and right leg simultaneously. The arm is raised higher than the head; the forehead remains parallel to the floor. This end position is maintained for a minimum of 10 seconds. Pay attention to regular breathing and tight abdominal muscles. Then repeat with the right arm and the left leg.

Variant

Advanced athletes raise both arms and both legs simultaneously. You can also intensify the exercise by holding dumbbells in your hands and attaching weights to your ankles.

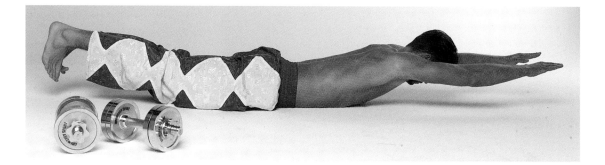

K **17**: Back Stretch from a Prone Position

> Strengthening:
> ++ Lower back muscles
> + Rear thigh muscles

Starting Position

Adjust the leg pads so that the pelvis can be moved freely. Wedge the feet against the foot pads, and place the hands next to the temples or across the upper body. Tighten the abdominal muscles for stabilization of the back.

Execution

Slowly and smoothly raise the upper body until your body forms a straight line. The entire move is generated by the back muscles. Briefly maintain the end position before you slowly return to the starting position. Avoid a swinging motion, and pay attention to a straight back and tight abdominal muscles.

Variant

Advanced athletes can intensify the exercise by holding dumbbells.

The Front and Rear Upper Arm Muscles

K **18**: Seated Biceps Curl

Strengthening:
++ Front upper arm muscles

Starting Position

Sit on a chair, with the arms lowered and close to the sides of the body. Hold dumbbells in your hands, with the palms facing each other. Extend your shoulders backward and tighten the abdominal muscles.

Execution

Alternately lift the lower arms, bending the elbows without changing the elbow position in relation to the body. In the process, the palm of the hand is turned up. In the end position, tense the front upper arm muscles at maximum strength for about three seconds while maintaining regular breathing. Then lower the arm slowly back to the starting position and start raising the other arm. Keep the wrists straight, and avoid pulling the shoulders forward.

K **19**: Concentration Curl

> **Strengthening:**
> **++ Front upper arm muscles**

Starting Position

Sit on a chair with your legs spread to the sides. Hold a dumbbell in your hand, with your elbow pressed against the inner part of your thigh and your palm pointing forward. Keep your shoulders back and tighten your abdominal muscles.

Execution

Move the dumbbell upward without changing the position of the elbow. In the end position, tense the front upper arm muscles at maximum strength for about three seconds while maintaining regular breathing. Then slowly return the lower arm to the starting position. However, the arm remains slightly bent and, because of this, the muscles remain tight. Keep your wrists straight and avoid pulling the shoulders forward to facilitate the exercise.

K **20**: Standing Biceps Curl

Strengthening: ++ Front upper arm muscles   + Front shoulder muscles

Starting Position

Stand upright with the legs slightly bent and hip-width apart. Hold a barbell in front of your thighs with your palms facing forward. The elbows are pressed against the body, and the shoulders are pushed backward. Tighten the abdominal muscles and the muscles of your buttocks.

Execution

Move the lower arms upward without changing the position of the elbows. In the end position, tense the front upper arm muscles at maximum strength for about three seconds while maintaining regular breathing. Then slowly extend the lower arms back down again, but not to a fully straight position, so that the muscles remain tight. Do not use a swinging motion, avoid bending the wrists, and do not move the shoulders forward to facilitate the exercise.

Variant

You can also carry out the exercise with dumbbells.

K **21**: Triceps Kickback

> **Strengthening:**
> **++ Rear upper arm muscles**

Starting Position

Take a lunge step and support yourself with one hand on your front thigh. Hold a dumbbell in the other hand. The upper arm is close to the body and the arm is bent; the abdominal muscles and the muscles of the buttocks are tight.

Execution

Straighten the arm, moving the lower arm only. Do not move the upper arm or use a swinging motion. Briefly maintain this position, then slowly return the lower arm to the starting position. Avoid turning the shoulders forward and do not bend the wrist.

Variant

For better stability you can support your weight with the front hand on a chair. The upper body will then be in a horizontal position.

You can also sit on a chair and move the dumbbell farther upward, for which you stabilize the position of the active arm with the help of the other arm. In that case, however, do not drop your lower arm much farther than to the horizontal position. Prior to all exercises that involve the dumbbell being above your head, always check the dumbbell collar carefully.

K 22: Dips

> **Strengthening:**
> ++ **Rear upper arm muscles**
> + **Shoulder muscles**

Starting Position

With your back to the ground, support yourself on your hands and the feet. The arms are nearly straight and the back is straight. The palms are touching the ground below the shoulders, with the fingers pointed toward the feet, and the feet are under the knees when the body is raised.

Execution

Bend the arms and, simultaneously, lower the buttocks, but do not rest them on the floor. Briefly maintain the end position before you return smoothly to the starting position.

Variant

The exercise can also be carried out on one or two objects, such as weight benches, dropping the weight farther and thus intensifying the exercise. For these variations, support yourself with your heels. Be careful to bend your arms only to the point where your upper arms are horizontal.

K 23: Cable Triceps Pulldown

> **Strengthening:**
> ++ Rear upper arm muscles

Starting Position

Face the rope pulley with the handle positioned up high. Pull the handle down until the upper and the lower arm roughly form a 90-degree angle. Keep your upper arm pressed to the side of the body and tense the abdominal muscles and the muscles of the buttocks.

Execution

Extend the lower arm down toward the thigh in a smooth movement until the arm is nearly straight. Maintain the position briefly before you slowly return the lower arm to the starting position. Avoid turning the shoulder to the front and do not bend the wrist.

Variant

You can also do this exercise with both arms—for example, with a V-grip.

The Abdominal Muscles

K 24: Crunch

> **Strengthening:**
> ++ Front abdominal muscles
> + Lateral abdominal muscles

Starting Position

Lie on your back, with the arms straight alongside the body, and the palms of the hands on the floor. The legs are bent and resting on the heels. Apply some pressure with your heels to the ground to avoid a hollow back during the exercise.

Execution

Slowly raise your upper body and, at the same time, pull the chin slightly toward the chest. The complete move is generated by the abdominal muscles, without a swinging motion. Hold the end position for about three seconds while you tighten the abdominal muscles at maximum strength and maintain regular breathing. Then slowly lower the upper body, but do not rest it on the floor, so that the muscles remain tight. Repeat the exercise.

Variant

To intensify the exercise you can hold a dumbbell disc on your chest. Advanced athletes can hold one dumbbell with both hands above the head during the exercise. Avoid a hollow back.

K **25**: Side Crunch

> **Strengthening:**
> ++ Front and lateral abdominal muscles

Starting Position

Lie on your back, with the legs bent and the heels on the ground. Lower the legs somewhat to one side, in order to achieve an initial tightness of the lateral abdominal muscles. Extend the hands, arms straight, to the opposite side, then raise the upper body in the direction of the hands.

Execution

Bring the arms sideways to the front, and raise the upper body to the same side. The entire move is generated by the abdominal muscles and without a swinging motion. Hold the end position for about three seconds, during which you tighten the abdominal muscles at full strength and maintain regular breathing. Then slowly lower the upper body, but do not rest on the floor, so that the muscles remain tight. After achieving the planned number of repetitions, carry out the exercise to the other side.

Variant

For intensification of this exercise you can place a dumbbell disc on your chest.

K **26**: Reverse Crunch

> **Strengthening:**
> ++ **Front abdominal muscles**
> + **Lateral abdominal muscles**

Starting Position

Sit on the floor with the legs bent and the feet resting on the heels. The knee joints form nearly a 90-degree angle. Tighten the abdominal muscles and slightly push the heels against the ground. The chin leans somewhat toward the chest.

Execution

Slowly and incrementally lower the upper body with the arms next to the body and somewhat above the ground. During the exercise, hold each position for 5–10 seconds, after which you lower the upper body farther. The movement to the ground position should take at least 60 seconds. Pay attention to regular breathing.

Variant

To intensify the exercise, do not rest the upper body on the floor, but raise it back up incrementally, which extends the exercise period by approximately two minutes.

Advanced athletes can place a dumbbell disc on their chest.

K **27**: Beetle

Strengthening:
++ Front and lateral abdominal muscles

Starting Position

Lie on your back with the arms straight and extending backward over the head. Raise the head and the out-stretched arms and legs away from the floor. Keep the lower back in contact with the floor.

Execution

Raise the upper body to the right. At the same time, pull the right knee toward the body and grip the inner side of the right foot with your left hand. Slowly return to the starting position, but do not rest the body on the floor. Then carry out the exercise to the left side. Avoid a swinging motion and a hollow back.

Variant

Beginners should hold the legs in a bent position, so that the lower leg and the thigh are at a 90-degree angle to each other. You can also keep your hands on the temples.

K 28: Plank

> **Strengthening:**
> ++ Front abdominal muscles
> + Lateral abdominal, front thigh, and shoulder muscles

Starting Position

In a prone position with the toes on the floor, support your weight with the lower arms so that the elbows are below the shoulder joints. Tighten the abdominal muscles.

Execution

Push your upper body upward until the legs and back are straight. Build up tension between the feet and elbows, and concentrate on activating the abdominal muscles. Maintain the end position for a minimum of 10 seconds. Pay attention to regular breathing, and avoid forming a hollow back.

Variant

Advanced athletes alternate raising the legs, keeping each leg up in the air for a few seconds.

K 29: Lateral Plank

> **Strengthening:**
> ++ **Lateral abdominal muscles**
> + **Front abdominal, outer thigh, and shoulder muscles**

Starting Position

You are in a side position with your elbow resting on the floor below the shoulder. The hip and the lower leg rest on the floor. Build up tension between the lower arm and the foot.

Execution

Raise the hips and the thigh so that only the outer side of the foot touches the floor. Maintain the position for a few seconds before you lower the hips, but not all the way down to the floor. Repeat the exercise. Pay attention to regular breathing, and avoid making compensatory twisting movements with the upper body.

Variant

You can intensify the exercise by raising the upper leg and extending your upper arm above the head. You can also hold a dumbbell, and use ankle weights.

K **30**: Side Bend

> **Strengthening:**
> ++ **Lateral abdominal muscles**
> + **Front abdominal and outer thigh muscles**

Starting Position

You are in a side position on the equipment, with the pad height adjusted so that you can move your upper body freely. Hold your hands against the temples with the elbows pointing outward. Slightly bend the upper body toward the floor.

Execution

Straighten the upper body in a smooth movement. Advanced athletes continue somewhat to the opposite side. Slowly return to the starting position. The entire move is generated by the lateral abdominal muscles. Avoid a swinging motion to facilitate the exercise, and do not make any compensatory movements with the hips or upper body.

Variant

Very advanced athletes can intensify the exercise by holding dumbbells.

CHAPTER 17

Strengthening Exercises for the Legs and Buttocks

This chapter will teach you the best strengthening exercises for the legs and buttocks. You will learn about exercises with dumbbells and barbells, bodyweight exercises, as well as exercises on machines. This way you can effectively exercise all your body's muscle groups, regardless of whether you are at home or at a fitness club. If suitable equipment is not available, switch to an exercise that activates the same muscle group.

Some muscle groups on the following pages have been combined for better clarity. More detailed information about the muscle functions can be found on pages 10–17.

Execution of the Exercises

Take the starting position and perform the exercise in accordance with the exercise description. Repeat the execution for as often as is required by the training method you use (see pp. 111–115). You must select a weight that permits technically correct repetitions—without wrong positioning or incorrect compensatory movements (see pp. 122–124). Advanced athletes can use intensifying techniques (see pp. 116–118). Although an exercise is described for only one side, the exercise should always be done on both sides so that both sides of the body are strengthened together.

The description of the exercises indicates whether the strengthening is of primary (++) or secondary (+) importance for the muscles.

> **The front thigh muscles and the gluteus muscles**
>
> **The rear thigh muscles**
>
> **The inner thigh muscles**
>
> **The outer thigh muscles**
>
> **The calf muscles**

The Front Thigh Muscles and the Gluteus Muscles

K 31: Squat

Strengthening:
++ Thigh muscles, particularly the front part, and gluteus muscles
 + Calf and lower back muscles

Starting Position

Stand upright with the knees slightly bent. Spread the feet apart a bit more than shoulder-width, and point the toes slightly outward. Hold dumbbells in your hands. Tighten the abdominal muscles and keep the back straight.

Execution

Bend the knees as low as possible and, in the process, shift your buttocks backward. Keep your back straight and keep the knees above the feet, not forward or to the side. Then straighten your legs, and lift your heels at the end of the move. Repeat the exercise.

Variant

The exercise can also be carried out with a barbell on the shoulders.

K **32**: Forward Lunge

> **Strengthening:**
> ++ **Front thigh and gluteus muscles**
> + **Inner, outer, and rear thigh and calf muscles**

Starting Position

Take a lunge step. The rear foot rests on the floor and the rear leg is supported by the toes throughout the exercise. Hold dumbbells in your hands with palms facing the body. Tighten the abdominal muscles and keep the upper body straight.

Execution

Bend both knees as low as possible, but do not rest the rear knee on the floor or change the position of your feet. Pay attention that the front knee remains above the foot, not forward or to the side. Straighten the legs, then repeat the exercise.

Variant

In place of dumbbells, hold a barbell on your shoulders.

K **33**: Bending One Leg

> **Strengthening:**
> ++ **Front thigh and gluteus muscles**
> + **Inner, outer, and rear thigh and calf muscles**

Starting Position

Stand upright on one leg with the other leg bent at the knee, with the foot off the ground and the sole of the foot pointing behind you. For a secure stance you must concentrate on the strain exerted on the ball, outer edge, and heel of the standing foot. Tighten the abdominal muscles and keep the back straight.

Execution

Slowly bend the standing leg until the thigh is horizontal, while shifting the buttocks backward so that the rear knee drops toward the

ground. Briefly maintain the position and do not rest the rear leg on the floor. Keep your back straight, and keep the knee above the foot, not forward or to the side. Then straighten the leg and, at the end of the exercise, raise the heel off the ground. Repeat the exercise.

Variant

Very advanced athletes carry out this exercise with the leg straight in the air to the front.

Very advanced athletes can also use dumbbells.

For training of takeoff power, jump off from the lower position. Return to the jump leg and repeat the exercise.

K **34**: Bending One Leg in a Fixed Position

> **Strengthening:**
> ++ Front thigh and gluteus muscles
> + Inner, outer, and rear thigh and calf muscles

Starting Position

Stand upright with one foot resting on a weight bench behind you. Hold dumbbells in your hands, palms facing the body. For a secure stance, concentrate on the strain exerted to the ball, outer edge, and heel of the standing foot. Tighten the abdominal muscles and keep the back straight.

Execution

Slowly bend the standing leg until the thigh is somewhat horizontal, and briefly maintain this position. Pay attention to a straight back, and keep the knee over the foot, not forward or to the side. Straighten the standing leg, and repeat the exercise.

Variant

For controlled learning, beginners can hold on to a chair to support their weight.

K 35: Leg Press

Strengthening:
++ Front thigh and gluteus muscles
+ Inner, outer, and rear thigh and calf muscles

Starting Position

Lie on the pad with the feet about shoulder-width apart and resting on a plate. The knee joints form an angle of about 90 degrees. Take hold of the handles and tighten the abdominal muscles for stabilization of the position.

Execution

Push the legs with steady power against the plate. Briefly maintain the end position before slowly returning to the starting position. Avoid raising your back away from the pad, and keep the knees in the leg axis, and not to the inside or outside.

Variant

When extending the legs you can also raise the heels. This has an intensifying effect on the calf muscles.

Changes in foot position will exercise different parts of the muscles. The higher the feet are, the more you will train the gluteus muscles instead of the thigh muscles.

K 36: Leg Extension

> Strengthening:
> ++ Front thigh muscles

Starting Position

Adjust the height of the seat and the leg pads in accordance with the size of your body. The rotary axis must be at the level of the knee joints, and the leg pads at the lower end of the shinbones. Lean back against the backrest, grip the handles, and tense the abdominal muscles for stabilization of the position.

Execution

Move the lower legs in a smooth movement upward until they are nearly straight. Then slowly return the lower legs to the starting position, but only to the extent that the muscles remain tight. Ensure that you do not form a hollow back.

Variant

The exercise can also be carried out with one leg.

The Rear Thigh Muscles

K 37: Leg Curl from a Prone Position

Strengthening:

++ Rear thigh muscles

 + Lower back and gluteus muscles

Starting Position

In a prone position, bend one leg slightly and keep the other leg straight. Put a knotted stretch band around the feet at medium tension. Tense the abdominal muscles.

Execution

Pull the bent leg as far as possible toward the buttocks and do not raise the other leg. Use a smooth movement and ensure that the pelvis remains on the floor. Then slowly return the leg to the starting position, but not beyond, so that the stretch band remains tense. Repeat the exercise.

Variant

You can also affix the stretch band to a low object, after which you pull the leg backward toward the buttocks and somewhat upward.

    You can also exercise these muscles standing up. With one foot, step on the stretch band and attach it around the heel of the other foot. Then pull the heel as far as possible toward the buttocks. Keep the thigh in a vertical position.

K **38**: Hip Lift

> **Strengthening:**
> ++ Rear thigh and gluteus muscles
> + Front thigh and lower back muscles

Starting Position

Lie on your back. Draw up the legs by bending the knees, and rest the heels on the floor. The knee joints form an angle of about 90 degrees. Tense the abdominal muscles and tighten the heels somewhat in the direction of the buttocks.

Execution

Push the heels hard against the ground and raise the hips so that the thighs and the back are in a straight line. Now lower and raise the hips several times without rest. In the process, you must pay attention to regular breathing and keep the abdominal muscles tight.

Variant

Advanced athletes can perform the exercise with one leg. For intensification the heel can be rested on an object—for example, a step.

If you exercise on the soles of your feet, instead of the heels, this will have a more pronounced effect on the front thigh muscles; however, it will be less intensive on the rear thigh muscles.

Furthermore, advanced athletes can put a dumbbell disc on the stomach and hold the disc in place with their hands.

K 39: Leg Curl from a Sitting Position

> **Strengthening:**
> ++ **Rear thigh muscles**

Starting Position

Adjust the height of the seat and leg pads in accordance with your body size. The rotary axis must be in line with the knee joints, and the leg pad close to the Achilles tendons. Bend the lower legs somewhat, so that the muscles experience a pre-tension. Rest your back fully against the cushion, and tense the abdominal muscles.

Execution

Move your lower legs in a smooth movement as far as possible in the direction of the buttocks. Then slowly return the lower legs to the starting position, but not beyond, so that the muscles remain tight. Make sure that you do not form a hollow back.

Variant

The exercise can also be carried out with one leg.

Types of equipment are available that enable the exercise to be done from a prone position. In a prone position the bending of the knees can also be carried out using a rope pulley.

The Inner Thigh Muscles

K 40: Side Position Adductor Exercise

Strengthening:
++ Inner thigh muscles

Starting Position

Lower yourself to the ground into a side position. The lower leg is straight and resting on the floor and the upper leg is bent with the sole of the foot on the floor in front of the body. You can support your head with the lower arm if necessary. The upper arm is in front of the body and resting on the floor to stabilize your position. Tighten the abdominal muscles and the muscles of the buttocks.

Execution

Raise the lower leg as far as you can and briefly maintain the end position. Keep the leg straight and the side of the foot parallel to the floor. Then lower the leg, but do not rest it on the ground, and repeat the exercise. Pay attention to a smooth and regular movement.

Variant

The exercise can be intensified with the use of ankle weights.

You can also put a dumbbell on the thigh to be exercised, holding the dumbbell in a fixed position with the hand. Heavy weights are not suitable in this case, as the pressure on the thigh causes pain.

K **41**: Drawing the Leg up in a Standing Position

> Strengthening:
> ++ Inner thigh muscles
> + Stabilizing muscles of the standing leg

Starting Position

Attach the stretch band to a low object at ankle-height, form a knot, and place the loops around the instep, on the inside of the foot. Hold on to the back of a chair, slightly bend the standing leg, and tighten the abdominal muscles for stabilization of your position. Draw the exercising leg somewhat up and keep it in the air, so that the band is slightly stretched and the muscles can feel some pre-tension.

Execution

Move the exercising leg in a smooth movement across the standing leg to the outside. Briefly maintain the position before returning the leg to the starting position, though not beyond, so that the muscles remain tight. Avoid a swinging motion, keep the body straight, and keep the abdominal muscles tight.

Variant

Exercising this muscle group is also possible using a rope pulley. To this end, affix the roller in the lower position and the rope with a foot sleeve to the exercising leg.

You can also do this exercise while standing on a step or a wooden board, so that the exercising leg can move freely.

The Outer Thigh Muscles

K 42: Side Position Leg Lift

> **Strengthening:**
> ++ **Outer thigh muscles**
> + **Gluteus muscles**

Starting Position

Get onto the ground in a side position, with the lower leg slightly bent and the upper leg straight and lying on the floor. With the lower arm you can support the head if necessary. The upper arm is in front of the body, palm against the floor, to stabilize your position. Tighten the abdominal muscles and the muscles of the buttocks.

Execution

Raise the upper leg high up in the air and stretch the heel while keeping the foot parallel to the ground. Then slowly move the leg back down, but not to the floor. Repeat the exercise. Pay attention to regular movements.

Variant

You can intensify the exercise with ankle weights.

Furthermore, you can put a dumbbell on the leg selected for training and hold it in place with your hand. Heavy weights are not suitable, as the pressure causes pain to the thigh.

K **43**: Standing Leg Lift

> **Strengthening:**
> **++ Outer thigh muscles**
>   **+ Stabilizing muscles of the standing leg**

Starting Position

Attach the stretch band to a low object at ankle-height, and form a loop for the outer foot (the foot farthest from the attached end of the stretch band). Support yourself on a chair, slightly bend the standing leg, and tighten the abdominal muscles for stabilization of your position. Raise the exercising leg slightly to the outside, so that the band is somewhat stretched, so the muscles experience pre-tension.

Execution

Move the exercising leg against the resistance in a smooth movement to the outside. Briefly maintain the end position before you return the leg to the starting position, but not beyond, so that the muscles remain tight. Avoid a swinging motion, and hold the upper body straight and the abdominal muscles tight.

Variant

Exercising this muscle group can also be carried out using a rope pulley. Affix the roller in a low position and attach the rope with a foot sleeve to your exercising leg.

   This can also be done on a step or a wooden board, so that the exercising leg can move freely.

The Calf Muscles

K 44: Heel Lift with Both Legs

Strengthening:
++ Calf muscles

Starting Position

Stand erect on a step, with your feet aligned with the hips and pointing forward. Let the arms hang down beside the body, and hold dumbbells in your hands, palms facing the body. Tighten the abdominal muscles and the muscles of the buttocks.

Execution

Raise the heels as much as possible and maintain this position for about three seconds. Then lower the heels, but do not rest them on the ground, and repeat the exercise. Perform the exercise without a swinging motion, as the movement must be generated exclusively by the calf muscles.

Variant

The exercise can also be carried out on the floor. However, this leaves little room for the maneuver, because the heels must not be lowered all the way down to the ground, so that the muscles remain tight.

K **45**: Heel Lift with One Leg

> **Strengthening:**
> **++ Calf muscles**

Starting Position

Stand erect on one leg, with the standing foot pointing forward. Let the arms hang down beside the body, and hold dumbbells in your hands, palms facing the body. Tighten the abdominal muscles and the muscles of the buttocks.

Execution

Raise the heel of the standing leg as much as possible and maintain the position for about three seconds. Then lower the heel, but do not rest it on the floor, and repeat the exercise. The exercise should not be carried out with a swinging motion, as the movement must be generated exclusively by the calf muscles.

Variant

Beginners carry out the exercise without dumbbells. You can use a chair to support your weight. After some practice, you will be able to perform the exercise without this support and press your hands against the hips.

Part V: Training Programs

CHAPTER **18**

Introduction

Regular fitness training improves your performance in martial arts. You will be able to deliver the techniques quickly and with power, and in training and competition you will be fit for longer periods. This requires separate sessions for stamina and power, which should be combined with flexibility training.

You will now learn how to organize a training session by yourself. To this end, the training must be divided into warm-up, main section, and cool-down. In addition, you will learn how to plan and monitor your training long term. For example, martial arts athletes who wish to improve their performance as quickly as possible for amateur fights can use the 10-week training plan. You will also be introduced to plans for advanced martial arts athletes.

CHAPTER 19

Structure of a Training Hour

Each type of sport is divided into the phases "warm-up," "main section," and "cool-down." Organize your training accordingly. The duration and organization of the phases depend on the priority, total duration, and intensity of the training.

1. Warm-up   **Duration: minimum 15 minutes**

1.1 Warm-up exercise

Exercise to warm up the body

1.2 Stretching

Preparatory stretching of the muscles

2. Main Section   **Duration: 30–90 minutes**

(depending on the type of sport)

2.1 Power training

Strengthening exercises for the upper body

or 2.2 Stamina training

Sport activity with regular intensity

or 2.3 Flexibility training

Intensive stretching of the muscles

3. Cool-down   **Duration: minimum 10 minutes**

3.1 Cool-down exercise

Exercise at low intensity

3.2 Stretching

Easy stretching of the activated muscles for regeneration

Warm-up

In the warm-up phase you prepare your body for the training session. This requires warming up and subsequent stretching. The body becomes fitter and is less prone to injuries.

Warm-up Exercise

Start the fitness training with an exercise that warms up the body and prepares it for the strain of training. Choose an exercise that can be carried out at a steady pace. The moves are carried out for 5–10 minutes. Do not lose your breath. Avoid extreme situations and do not perform any quick or rapid moves. This phase is meant to get your body adjusted to the training, and not to achieve maximum performance.

For example, you can warm up with easy jogging. If you exercise at home, it is recommended that you walk or jog on the spot. Suitable training equipment could be a cycle ergometer, a jump rope, or a step.

Stretching

Stamina and power training in the main section require prior stretching. However, if stretching forms the main section, the stretching in the warm-up phase will not be necessary.

Once you have warmed up your body, start with the stretching exercises. It is best to intensively stretch all the muscle groups. In order to reduce the length of the training session, it will also suffice to stretch those muscle groups that will be activated in the main section. Without prior stretching, there will be a risk of injury, and the body will not be properly prepared for the exercise and thus will not be able to deliver maximum performance.

Plan a minimum of five minutes for the preparatory stretching of individual muscle groups. However, the time can be extended, particularly if you wish to improve your flexibility.

Main Section

The warm-up phase is followed by the main section of fitness training. This section involves mainly power training or stamina training. You can also carry out a session in which you concentrate on flexibility training. In addition, you can add coordination exercises, such as the "one-leg stand," to the training session (see pp. 198–199). However, a complete training session in the main section including coordination exercises becomes necessary only after serious injuries.

Power Training

Beginners exercise in the initial training sessions according to the stamina power method. Carry out many repetitions of the exercises at low intensity. This is meant to get your body used to the new types of moves. For optimum results, learn to focus the attention on the activated muscles. After a familiarization phase of a few weeks, choose between the stamina power and muscle development methods (see pp. 112–113).

Stamina Training

The initial training sessions are dedicated to the basic stamina. Gradually improve the stamina by extending your training time in each session. You will already notice clear progress after a few training sessions, provided you train at least twice a week. The aim is to be able to run a minimum of 40 minutes without a break at a low pulse rate. Once you have been successful at this, you can turn to more intensive types of stamina training, such as fitness stamina sessions and interval training. However, continue to include sessions for basic stamina (see pp. 91–92).

Flexibility Training

You can also carry out training sessions dedicated solely to flexibility training. This entails a stretching program for the whole body. Select at least one exercise for each muscle group. To be able to achieve intensive stretch positions, you can perform several exercises for each muscle group. However, do not attempt to attain a position by force, as this leads to a hardening of the muscles and can cause injury (see pp. 39–40).

Cool-down

In the cool-down phase the training is concluded by cooling the body down and doing some stretching exercises for the activated muscles. Regeneration measures, such as a massage and taking a bath in warm water, are recommended. This helps the body to relax and to reduce the tension, thus accelerating regeneration. After an intensive training session, you should also plan for an additional hour of sleep, which the body requires for regeneration.

Cool-down Exercise

After a training session, you should cool down to relax the muscles. This also helps the body to regenerate quickly. Move at an easy pace for a few minutes, without effort. Particularly suitable are walking, slow jogging, and cycling at low intensity. Continue for about five minutes.

Stretching

At the end of your fitness training, stretch the activated muscles once more. Do not move into any extreme stretch positions, as the muscles are tired and tend to cramp. Limit the stretching to the first stretch phase, and do not extend the position thereafter (see pp. 35–37). The stretching at the end of training serves to loosen the muscles and to prevent shrinking of the muscles.

The One-Leg Stand

The one-leg stand is a reasonable way to develop coordination. You can always include this exercise during the warm-up phase of training sessions.

Stand up straight and keep one leg in the air. Slightly bend the standing leg, and press the hands against the hips. Support your weight with the heel, the outer side of the foot, and the ball of the foot of the standing leg. Keep your shoulders straight, and do not pull up a shoulder for balance. Monitor your position regularly in front of a mirror.

✖ A: The one-leg stand with open eyes.
✖ B: The one-leg stand with closed eyes and slow head turns to the right and left.

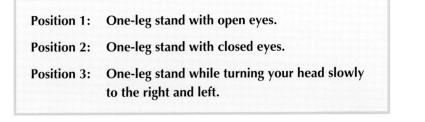

Position 1:	One-leg stand with open eyes.
Position 2:	One-leg stand with closed eyes.
Position 3:	One-leg stand while turning your head slowly to the right and left.

Training

Start your training with position 1. If you succeed in maintaining the position for 15 seconds, close your eyes (position 2). Should you also succeed in maintaining this position for approximately 15 seconds, slowly turn your head right and left (position 3). Then do the one-leg stand with the other leg.

As a variant to the training you can swing your raised leg in all directions. Very advanced athletes are able to keep the straightened leg in the air.

✖ The perfect one-leg stand.

CHAPTER 20

Planning and Monitoring of Training

Divide your training into cycles of 6–12 weeks each. On conclusion of one cycle, determine a program for the next cycle. It is recommended to proceed as shown:

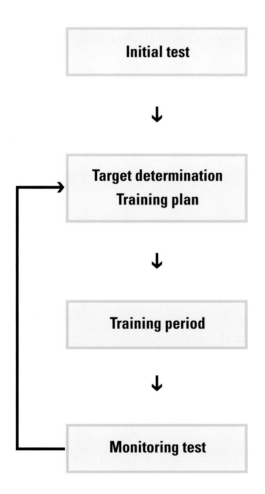

Initial Test

Prior to your training program, check for *injuries* that require a medical examination. The next step establishes the *current values:* determine your weight, percentage of body fat, and body measurements and record the results in your training journal. You will monitor the success of your training program on the basis of these records. In addition, you can use the journal to take notes on your sport-specific performance level and on your flexibility, power, and stamina.

Target Determination and Training Plan

Next, define your *training targets* by using the results determined in the initial test. Be aware of what you are trying to achieve by the martial arts and fitness training. You must also record how much time you can allocate to the training and what you expect to achieve with this training effort. Your training targets should be based on these considerations, taking into account the initial test results. Remain realistic to avoid disappointment and failure. The targets are divided into short-, medium-, and long-term aspirations, as the achievement of a short-term target provides the motivation to continue.

In line with these fundamentals, determine the *training program,* which should contain sessions for the fitness components of power, stamina, and flexibility. Exercise with this program for a period of 6–12 weeks. After a training period of 6 weeks, you will be able to see the success. However, you should not use the same program for more than 12 weeks, so that the body receives ever new training stimuli and to avoid stagnation of performance. At the end of the predetermined training phase, you must either vary and change the exercises in the program or create a new program. When planning training programs for the fitness component of power, you must ensure that all the important muscle groups (see pp. 10–17) are intensively strengthened at least once a week.

Training Period

After target definition and program determination, commence the training period of 6–12 weeks. The *power exercises* in the first training sessions should be carried out at low weight/intensity. The body must first get used to the new moves. To avoid injuries, do not increase the weights/intensity too fast. Stay away from excessive strain in *stamina training.* Instead, you should gradually increase the length of the training tracks. In *stretching exercises,* pay attention to careful positioning, to avoid the risk of injuries. After each training session, make notes in your *training journal.* In this way you will be able to monitor your performance level for an extended period of time.

Monitoring Test

Success in training must be determined by regular monitoring tests. To this end, the criteria of the initial test must be reexamined. Such a test is recommended every 4 weeks. In addition, conclude each training phase with a monitoring test, and compare these test results with those of the initial test. Based on these test comparisons, and keeping in mind the training targets, modify the training program and—if necessary—the training targets.

Motivation

In the course of a training program you will always have certain phases in which you experience a lack of motivation. This applies particularly to the initial training sessions, when the body is not yet used to the sport activity. Lack of motivation entails the risk of falling back into the old rhythm (without training). Therefore, you should organize your training so that it does not get boring. Vary power exercises and the stamina training routes, change the training partners, and make use of stimulating music. Looking through your training journal will also help.

Look up the reasons why you started the training and remember the targets you set for yourself. Consider what you have reached so far and ask yourself whether it makes sense to stop.

The longer you are in training, the less you will experience difficulties in motivation. Even after a short break from training, your body will again yearn for exercise and the subsequent feeling of happiness and satisfaction.

✖ With regular fitness training, you optimize your performance level in your martial arts—as has Martin Albers (World and European Champion in Kick-Boxing).

CHAPTER 21

The Correct Fight Weight

To become eligible for competition you and your trainer must determine a weight division, and then concentrate your training on this weight. Many factors must be considered in the determination of the best-suited weight division, such as the current weight, the percentage of body fat, the fight style, and the competitive situation.

The percentage of body fat should be as low as possible, 8–10 percent for professional athletes. The percentage of body fat can be somewhat higher in amateurs, who do not have to face the same demands. A high degree of fat means that the athlete is not fully trained. Therefore, the athlete must compete in a higher weight division, in which the opponents will be stronger. In this situation, athletes can survive only if they are technically clearly superior.

If the athlete's percentage of body fat is 15 percent, body fat can be reduced to about 6 percent by intensive training and the correct nutrition. At a weight of 170 pounds this means a reduction in body fat of 10.2 pounds without loss of performance. Further slimming can be achieved only by a reduction in muscle mass, which leads to less strength and a deterioration in performance. Experience shows that it gets progressively more difficult to lose body fat the closer you come to the optimal area. For example, it is easier to achieve a reduction from 15 to 13 percent than from 12 to 10 percent.

If you want to keep track of your body's development, you can check your weight, the percentage of body fat, and the body's dimensions at regular intervals. Record the results in your training journal. The notes highlight the success in training. The procedure is also recommended if you do not wish to participate in competition, but only want to concentrate on the fitness aspects.

Determination of Body Fat

The measuring system for body fat determines the percentage of fat in relation to the body's weight. Do regular checks and record the results. Thus, you will be able to monitor success in training over an extended period of time. If, instead, you only keep track of your weight, it will be difficult to assess your success. Even though you build up your muscles and eliminate many pads of fat, you will not experience a significant difference in weight in the following months because the new sports activity at the beginning of a training program leads to the development of muscles and reduces the fat. However, the fat is lighter than the muscles. Even if you start off overweight, you will experience a loss in weight, as significant developments of muscle mass can be achieved only by intensive power training. The measurement of fat provides you with the opportunity to check, during the course of each training section, whether the percentage of body fat has been reduced.

The percentage of fat can be determined with a pair of calipers. A special weight scale, which includes a fat measurement device, results in a more accurate determination. These scales operate on the basis

of the bioelectric impedance analysis (BIA). This involves the transmission of a harmless, weak electric current through the body. As the conductivity of fat is not as high as the conductivity of muscles and other tissues, the percentage of body fat can be measured by the resistance (impedance). Weight scales of this type are available in the trade for approximately $100 and up.

Checklist for Body Measurement

For assessment of your body's development you can measure the individual body sections at regular intervals. Measure the size of the upper arms, chest, waist, hips, thighs, and calves, as these parts show the clearest changes. The aim is to achieve a narrow waist, while the other parts increase in size. Accordingly, examine the waist at its most narrow point and all other parts at their largest point. Record the results on a checklist.

However, the primary aim of competitive athletes who are above their weight limit despite a relatively low percentage of fat is to reduce the size of the waist and to maintain or slightly reduce the size of the other body parts.

Take the measurements at regular time intervals—for example, every four weeks. If you find out in the process that you did not succeed with your training targets, you must either change your program or determine new, more realistic targets. However, you should not examine your proportions too often, as the pressure on your performance may be too high.

The test must always be carried out at the same time of the day, to avoid inaccuracy of the test results. Conducting the test in the morning before breakfast is recommended.

	Initial Test
Date	
Weight	
Body fat	
1. *right upper arm*	
2. *left upper arm*	
3. *chest center*	
4. *waist*	
5. *hips*	
6. *right thigh*	
7. *left thigh*	
8. *right calf*	
9. *left calf*	

Nutritional Target: Maintaining the Fight Weight

Do you want to improve your performance, but wish to hold on to your fight weight? In the course of your martial arts oriented training, as in your stamina and power training, ensure that caloric intake corresponds to caloric consumption. Adopt healthy eating habits with low-fat meat products, fish, whole-grain products, fruit, fresh vegetables, and high-quality fats.

Do not exercise on an empty stomach. Consume sufficient carbohydrates and protein. It is best to eat your biggest meal approximately three hours prior to training and to eat a carbohydrate-rich snack, such as a banana, about an hour before you start. You will then be able to call on your optimum performance during training. It is also worthwhile to eat a fitness bar in the course of a power training session. Drinking lots of fluids during training is recommended—for example, an apple-juice mix containing one-third apple juice and two-thirds mineral water. After the training session, concentrate on foods rich in carbohydrates and protein, so that the body receives the nutrients required for regeneration.

Food Guidelines
- Nutrients geared toward optimal caloric consumption.
- High-grade carbohydrates.
  Whole-grain products are best.
- Moderate proportion of protein.
  Low-fat meat products, legumes (peas and beans), turkey, and fish are best.
- Moderate amounts of fat.
  High-quality fats with simple unsaturated fatty acids and omega-3 fatty acids are best.
- Plenty of fluids.
  Mineral water, apple-juice mix, and energy drinks during training.
- Use food supplements to promote quicker regeneration, but this is not essential.

Nutritional Target: Reducing Body Fat

Do you want to reduce your body fat to be able to compete in a lower weight division? This can be achieved if you add to your martial arts oriented training, stamina, and fitness sessions while consuming fewer calories than what the body uses up. In order not to lose valuable muscle mass, you must considerably increase the proportion of protein in your diet and decrease the proportion of carbohydrates accordingly. Pay attention to low-fat nutrition, but do not neglect high-quality fats. It is also important to drink plenty of fluids.

Two to three hours before training, eat food rich in protein—for example, a protein shake—and one to two hours before training, eat food rich in carbohydrates—for example, a banana. This is of particular importance prior to power training; otherwise, you will feel drained. After the training session, return to nutrition rich in carbohydrates and protein. However, the amount of carbohydrates should not be too much, so that the calorie-burning effect of training is not offset. Do not abstain from carbohydrates completely, as this would have a negative effect on the protein in the muscles.

Food Guidelines

- Caloric intake lower than caloric consumption.
- Low proportion of carbohydrates.
  Choose products with a low glycogen index, and choose whole-grain products as often as possible.
- High proportion of protein.
  Turkey, low-fat cheese and cottage cheese, whey, legumes, and fish are best.
- Low proportion of fat.
  High-quality fats containing simple unsaturated fatty acids are best.
- High intake of fluids, especially mineral water.
- Consuming amino-acid supplements helps to maintain the muscle mass but is not essential.

Nutritional Target: Increasing Muscle Size

Do you want to increase the size of your muscles significantly to be able to compete in a higher weight division? This requires thorough muscle buildup training combined with an increase in calories, predominantly made up of protein. So that you do not increase the proportion of body fat at the same time, you must pay attention to low-fat nutrition. This will not have an adverse effect on the supply of fat, as you will increase the food intake in general.

Two to three hours before the power training, consume a meal rich in protein—for example, a protein shake with oatmeal—and one to two hours before training, a carbohydrate-rich snack—for example, a fitness bar. During training you must drink plenty of fluids. Eating a protein bar is also recommended, so that the protein is available to the body immediately after training. Subsequent to the training session, start to refill the empty carbohydrate battery and consume more protein at the same time. You should also eat plenty of protein-rich foods on days without power training, so that the body receives sufficient protein for muscle development.

Food Guidelines

- Higher caloric intake in the buildup phase.
- Somewhat increased supply of carbohydrates.
  Noodles, rice, and fitness bars are best.
- High protein requirement.
  Protein (whey) shakes, protein bars, fish, lean meat like
  turkey, low-fat cottage cheese, and legumes are best.
- Low proportion of fat.
- High intake of fluids, especially mineral water.
- Amino-acid and creatine supplements can be taken for muscle buildup,
  but these are not essential.

	I	M 1	M 2	M 3	M 4	M 5	M 6
Date							
Weight							
Body fat							
1. right upper arm							
2. left upper arm							
3. chest center							
4. waist							
5. hips							
6. right thigh							
7. left thigh							
8. right calf							
9. left calf							

CHAPTER **22**

Training Journal

Maintain a training journal to monitor the development of your body over an extended period of time. Start the journal when you start your training program. The notes will eventually be very helpful, as they record the reasons for success and failure in training. The records will lead to better understanding of your body and how it reacts to changes. This information will help you to organize a more effective training program in the future.

Use a large ring binder as the training journal, so that you can add sheets of paper. You can use a computer to create the pages in accordance with your own ideas.

Body Measurement Test

Start with an initial test (see pp. 206–208). Record the results in your journal and repeat the test at regular intervals. You can devise a plan covering 6 months, for example. First, note the results of the initial test (I), and repeat the test each month (M x). This will clearly show the development of your body.

Training Targets

Be aware of what you wish to achieve by your fitness training and take a note of your training targets. Note short-, medium-, and long-term targets. At the beginning of each new training cycle (see pp. 201–203), record the short-term training targets—those that will clearly indicate improvement of a certain power performance.

	Training Targets	Results Achieved
Start of training		
Training Cycle 1		
Training Cycle 2		
Training Cycle 3		

Improve the understanding of your body and learn how it reacts to training stimuli and changes in training, so that you can plan and organize your training in the best possible way. The better you achieve this, the faster you will be able to reach your training targets.

Plans for the Training Period

After each training session, you should collate details on the performance achieved. Record, for example, what you concentrated on in martial arts training, or what performance you achieved in fitness training. To this end, you must record in stamina training the distance, training time, and average pulse rate, and in power training the exercises, dumbbell weights, number of sets, and number of repetitions.

It also makes sense to include the framework conditions of the training, as the athletic performance is influenced by factors such as stress, nutrition, and sleep.

The following plans are merely suggestions. Adapt these examples to your own athletic requirements, and include your plans in your training journal.

Martial Arts Training Plan		
Date:	11/7/06	
Duration:	90 min	
Focal point:	Combinations of three techniques—for example, jab, straight punch, and round kick	
Shadow boxing:	3 rounds	
Sandbag training:	3 rounds	
Pad training:	4 rounds	
Partner training:	20 min	
Sparring:	5 min	
Notes:	Too tired for intensive sparring	

Stamina Training Plan

Date:	*11/8/06*		
Type of sport:	*Jogging*		
Duration:	*40 min*		
Intensity:	*150–155 HR*		
Notes:	*Nothing special*		

The preceding plan is an example of a program covering the entire body. The weights shown are representative for a male athlete who has already been training with the intensity of an advanced athlete in accordance with the muscle development method for a few months, and who has progressively increased the weights. Do not consider the weights as starting weights, as they are much too heavy. However, you will be surprised to see how much your strength improves after 12 months of training.

Power Training Plan

Date:	11/9/06		
Exercise:	Sets and repetitions Weight	Sets and repetitions Weight	Sets and repetitions Weight
K 1: Bench Press	2 x 12 75 pounds per dumbbell		
K 11: One-Armed Dumbbell Row	2 x 12 80 pounds		
K 6: Overhead Press	2 x 11 45 pounds per dumbbell		
K 18: Seated Biceps Curl	2 x 10 40 pounds per dumbbell		
K 21: Triceps Kickback	2 x 12 35 pounds		
K 31: Squat	2 x 10 70 pounds per dumbbell		
K 38: Hip Lift	2 x 11 20-pound disc		
K 24: Crunch	2 x 12 50-pound disc		
K 15: Leaning the Upper Body Forward	2 x 12 20 pounds per dumbbell		
Notes:	Nothing special		

CHAPTER 23

Program for Beginners

You will soon succeed with performance improvements if you practice your martial arts type of sport three times a week. If you plan to participate in competitive fights, you have to include additional training sessions for stamina and power. Fitness training enables you to perform the techniques with greater power and to stay fit longer during competition and training.

In the amateur area, good results are achieved by six training sessions per week, and even high competitive aims can be reached. However, this is based on the assumption that you do not have to lose much weight prior to the contest to compete in your weight division. In such a situation, even an amateur must add to the six sessions.

You must continue to alter and change your training plan, as this provides new stimuli for the body. Once the body gets used to the demands and the training becomes monotonous, the performance will stagnate. Against this backdrop, you should always determine training cycles of 6–12 weeks with slightly different targets, such as the 10-week cycle described next. At the end of the cycle, resume training in accordance with a slightly changed plan. It is best to record your training plans and performance in a training journal so that you are able to monitor the development of your physical performance over an extended period of time.

10-Week Cycle

This program covers 10 weeks. Use it to further your fitness, thereby attaining better results in martial arts. The basic stamina is developed during the first few weeks. The stamina is preserved in the following weeks and the power training is intensified.

Weeks 1 to 6

The goal is to improve performance in martial arts, to which end three sessions are carried out per week. After the body has become accustomed to the power training, previously achieved fitness is maintained with one session per week.

Weeks 7 to 10

The intensity of the martial arts training is maintained. The primary aim in stamina training is to maintain the basic stamina, for which one session per week is sufficient. The power training is increased to two sessions per week.

Break. A day of rest for regeneration of the body.

F = Flexibility. The main part of training is concentrated on flexibility.

M = Martial arts. The session is dedicated to martial arts training. This training also has an effect on flexibility, particularly due to the extensive stretch program in the warm-up phase. In addition, you train for power, particularly resilience power. You can also include some power exercises in the cool-down phase.

P = Power. The session is reserved for power training. The whole body program A, which is made up of basic exercises (see pp. 232–233), is recommended.

S = Stamina. The session is reserved for stamina training—for example, jogging.

	Day 1	Day 2	Day 3	Day 4	Day 5	Day 6	Day 7
Week 1	M	S	M	P	F	M	Break
Week 2	M	S	M	P	F	M	Break
Week 3	M	S	M	P	S	M	Break
Week 4	M	S	M	P	S	M	Break
Week 5	M	S	M	P	S	M	Break
Week 6	M	S	M	P	S	M	Break
Week 7	M	P	M	S	P	M	Break
Week 8	M	P	M	S	P	M	Break
Week 9	M	P	M	S	P	M	Break
Week 10	M	P	M	S	P	M	Break

CHAPTER **24**

Program for Advanced Fighters

Advanced fighters exercise in accordance with individual training programs that are tailored to their particular requirements—for example, preparing for the next fight. Professional athletes frequently prepare themselves for a contest with a 12-week training plan. The trainer develops a program once the opponent and the framework conditions of the fight have been agreed upon. In the process, the necessary weight reduction and the opponent's fight style come into consideration. Training cycles during periods without competitive fights are used to eliminate the fighter's weak points, or to change the proportions of the body so that the athlete can compete in a more suitable weight division.

Advanced athletes must also divide their training into cycles of 6–12 weeks (see pp. 201–203). The training requires exact planning and detailed journaling of the sessions, as it will become increasingly difficult to improve the performance. The body must continually be confronted with new stimuli. This is the only way to achieve improvements.

During preparation of the training program, ensure that it includes martial arts oriented training, stamina training at different intensities, and power training for all muscle groups. Even though the programs have different priorities, efforts must be made to maintain the performance levels in areas not shown as a priority. For fitness training, this requires a minimum of one stamina and one power training session with a whole body program once per week.

Training Program: Muscle Development

This program shows how advanced martial arts athletes can arrange a training cycle if they plan to increase their muscle mass without increasing the proportion of body fat. Proper nutrition is essential (see p. 211).

At the end of the program, a new training program will be used.

Day 1. Stamina training unit (S) in the morning—for example, jogging for 40–60 minutes. Martial arts training (M) in the afternoon.

Day 2. Intensive power training (P). The sessions alternate weekly between training for the upper body (power program B) and for the legs (power program C).

Day 3. Stamina training unit (S) in the morning—for example, jogging for 40–60 minutes. Martial arts training (M) in the afternoon.

Day 4. Intensive power training (P). The sessions alternate weekly between training for the legs (power program C) and for the upper body (power program B).

Day 5. The day is solely dedicated to martial arts training (M). Sparring forms a major part of the training.

Day 6. Intensive power training (P). The units alternate weekly between training for the upper body (power program B) and for the legs (power program C).

Day 7. Break for regeneration.

	Day 1	Day 2	Day 3	Day 4	Day 5	Day 6	Day 7
Week 1	S (TU 1) + M (TU 2)	PB	S (TU 1) + M (TU 2)	PC	M Sparring	PB	Break
Week 2	S (TU 1) + M (TU 2)	PC	S (TU 1) + M (TU 2)	PB	M Sparring	PC	Break
Week 3	S (TU 1) + M (TU 2)	PB	S (TU 1) + M (TU 2)	PC	M Sparring	PB	Break
Week 4	S (TU 1) + M (TU 2)	PC	S (TU 1) + M (TU 2)	PB	M Sparring	PC	Break
Week 5	S (TU 1) + M (TU 2)	PB	S (TU 1) + M (TU 2)	PC	M Sparring	PB	Break
Week 6	S (TU 1) + M (TU 2)	PC	S (TU 1) + M (TU 2)	PB	M Sparring	PC	Break
Week 7	S (TU 1) + M (TU 2)	PB	S (TU 1) + M (TU 2)	PC	M Sparring	PB	Break
Week 8	S (TU 1) + M (TU 2)	PC	S (TU 1) + M (TU 2)	PB	M Sparring	PC	Break

Note: TU = Training Unit

Training Program: Improving the Martial Arts Performance

This intensive program is aimed primarily at improvement of the martial arts performance. A healthy and balanced diet is essential. It is also worthwhile to use food supplements, which further the regeneration (see p. 209).

   The program is scheduled for 6 weeks. Subsequently, reduce the intensity somewhat and use a new training program.

Day 1. Stamina training unit (S) in the morning—for example, jogging for 40–60 minutes. Martial arts training (M) in the afternoon.

Day 2. Power training unit (P) in the morning, for which a whole body program (A) is carried out. Martial arts training (M) in the afternoon.

Day 3. The day is solely dedicated to martial arts training (M). Sparring forms a major part of the training.

Day 4. Stamina training unit (S) in the morning—for example, jogging for 40–60 minutes. Martial arts training (M) in the afternoon.

Day 5. Power training unit (P) in the morning, for which a whole body program (A) is carried out. Martial arts training (M) in the afternoon.

Day 6. The day is solely dedicated to martial arts training (M). Sparring forms a major part of the training.

Day 7. Break for regeneration.

	Day 1	Day 2	Day 3	Day 4	Day 5	Day 6	Day 7
Week 1	S (TU 1) + M (TU 2)	PA (TU 1) + M (TU 2)	M Sparring	S (TU 1) + M (TU 2)	PA (TU 1) + M (TU 2)	M Sparring	Break
Week 2	S (TU 1) + M (TU 2)	PA (TU 1) + M (TU 2)	M Sparring	S (TU 1) + M (TU 2)	PA (TU 1) + M (TU 2)	M Sparring	Break
Week 3	S (TU 1) + M (TU 2)	PA (TU 1) + M (TU 2)	M Sparring	S (TU 1) + M (TU 2)	PA (TU 1) + M (TU 2)	M Sparring	Break
Week 4	S (TU 1) + M (TU 2)	PA (TU 1) + M (TU 2)	M Sparring	S (TU 1) + M (TU 2)	PA (TU 1) + M (TU 2)	M Sparring	Break
Week 5	S (TU 1) + M (TU 2)	PA (TU 1) + M (TU 2)	M Sparring	S (TU 1) + M (TU 2)	PA (TU 1) + M (TU 2)	M Sparring	Break
Week 6	S (TU 1) + M (TU 2)	PA (TU 1) + M (TU 2)	M Sparring	S (TU 1) + M (TU 2)	PA (TU 1) + M (TU 2)	M Sparring	Break

Note: TU = Training Unit

CHAPTER 25

Stretching and Strengthening Programs

Each training session starts with the *warm-up phase.* Carry out a warm-up exercise for 5–10 minutes at a steady pace. At the fitness club you can use, for example, a cycle ergometer. For your training at home you can walk or jog in place. Then stretch the muscles. Stretching all muscle groups once, and the weak points intensively, is recommended. However, you can shorten the stretching period by stretching only those primary muscle groups that will be activated in the main section of the training.

Then start the *main training section.* This can be power training or a stamina type of sport. You can also carry out stretching as the main part of your training. To this end, perform each exercise of the following whole body program two to three times. Furthermore, you can add exercises for muscle groups to improve your flexibility.

Finish the training with the *cool-down phase.* To cool down, carry out an exercise at very low intensity, for approximately five minutes. Afterward, once again stretch the primary muscle groups that were activated in the main training section (see pp. 193–197).

Strengthening Programs

The programs have been devised so that they can be carried out at a fitness club and at home. The exercises and the variants can be done using small pieces of equipment and on fitness machines.

Stretching Program—Example

The stretching program can be used as a start-up to your own martial arts training. Adapt the program to your individual requirements in line with your progress in training, your experience, and improved fitness.

✖ D 1: Leaning the Head Sideways, D 3: Pushing the Chest Forward, D 11: Lateral Bending of the Upper Body, D 5: Lateral Arm Push to the Rear, D 8: Holding Hands Behind the Back, D 14: Calf Stretch Alternating Between Straight and Bent Leg, D 19: Stretching the Leg in the Air, D 17: Lunge, D 18: Rear Thigh Stretch Bending Upper Body Forward, D 21: Straddle Stand, D 22: Front Bend of the Upper Body from a Straddle Position, D 23: Body Rotation in a Sitting Position.

Power Program A: Whole Body

Warm-up exercises and stretching (whole body program—see pp. 230–231)

1. **K 1:** Bench Press or **K 3:** Push-up or **K 4:** Chest Press on a Machine

2. **K 11:** One-Armed Dumbbell Row or **K 13:** Lateral Pulldown or **K 14:** Chin-up

3. **K 6:** Overhead Press or **K 7:** Lateral Raises

4. **K 31:** Squat or **K 35:** Leg Press

5. **K 38:** Hip Lift on heels or **K 37:** Leg Curl from a Prone Position

6. **K 24:** Crunch or **K 26:** Reverse Crunch or **K 27:** Beetle

7. **K 29:** Lateral Plank or **K 30:** Side Bend

8. **K 16:** Raising the Body from a Prone Position or **K 17:** Back Stretch from a Prone Position

Cool-down exercises and stretching

Two to three sets   8–12 or 15–20 repetitions per set (depending on the training target)

Static exercise **K 16:** 30–60 seconds per set

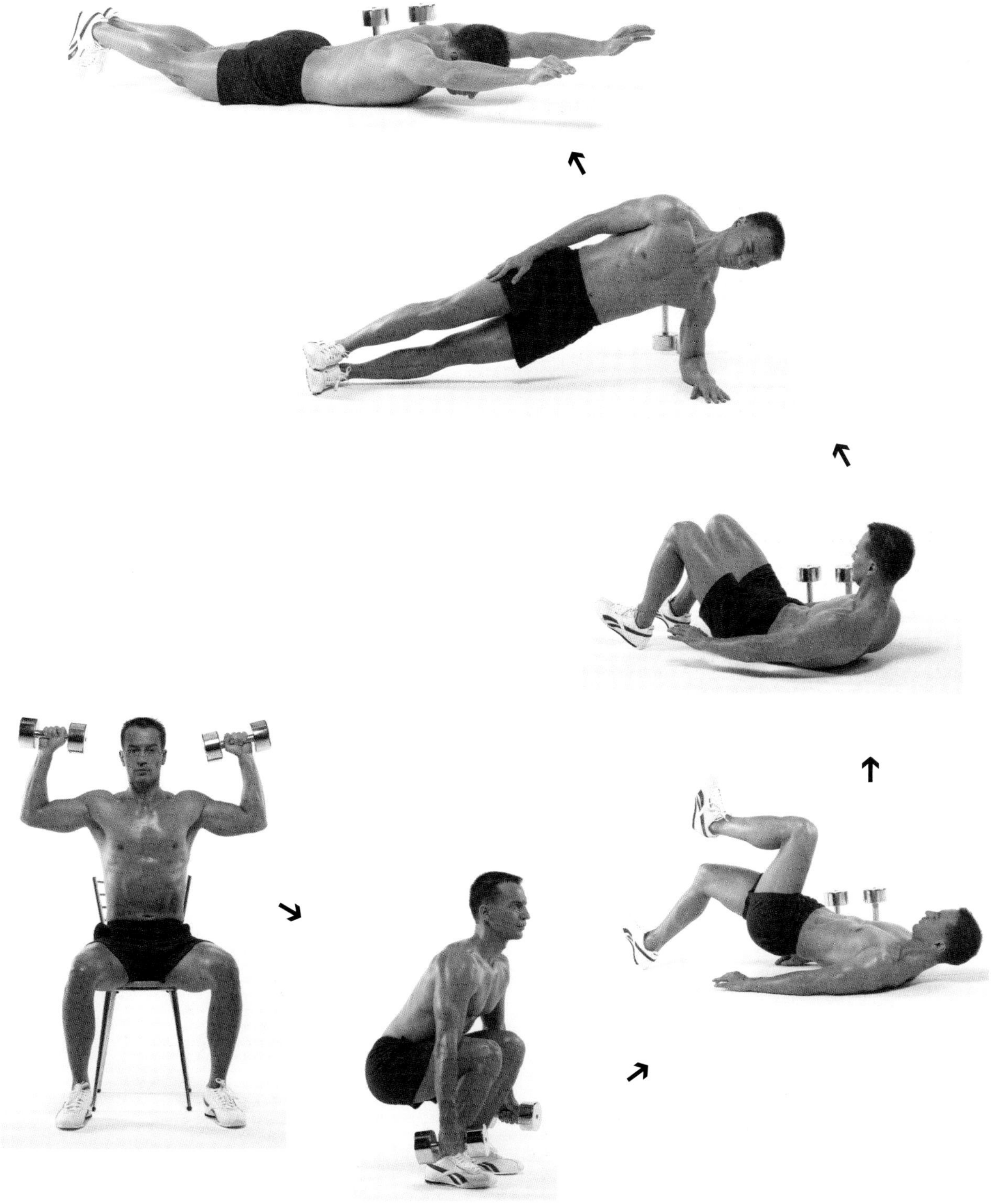

✖ K 1, K 11, K 6, K 31, K 38, K 24, K 29, K 16

Power Program B: Upper Body

Warm-up exercises and stretching (whole body program—see pp. 230–231—or upper body program)

1. **K 3**: Push-up or **K 1**: Bench Press or **K 4**: Chest Press on a Machine

2. **K 2**: Flies Lying on the Back or **K 5**: Flies on a Machine

3. **K 12**: Dumbbell Row with Both Arms or **K 13**: Lateral Pulldown or **K 14**: Chin-up

4. **K 8**: Reverse Flies or **K 10**: Reverse Flies on a Machine

5. **K 6**: Overhead Press or **K 7**: Lateral Raises

6. **K 18**: Seated Biceps Curl or **K 19**: Concentration Curl or **K 20**: Standing Biceps Curl

7. **K 21**: Triceps Kickback or **K 23**: Cable Triceps Pulldown

8. **K 26**: Reverse Crunch or **K 28**: Plank or **K 24**: Crunch

9. **K 29**: Lateral Plank or **K 30**: Side Bend

10. **K 15**: Leaning the Upper Body Forward or **K 17**: Back Stretch from a Prone Position

Cool-down exercises and stretching

Two to three sets   8–12 or 15–20 repetitions per set (depending on the training target)

✖ K 3, K 2, K 12, K 8, K 6, K 18, K 21, K 26, K 29, K 15

Power Program C: Legs and Buttocks

Warm-up exercises and stretching (whole body program—see pp. 230–231—or legs, buttocks, and torso program)

1. **K 31:** Squat or **K 34:** Bending One Leg in a Fixed Position

2. **K 32:** Forward Lunge or **K 36:** Leg Extension

3. **K 37:** Leg Curl from a Prone Position or **K 39:** Leg Curl from a Sitting Position

4. **K 40:** Side Position Adductor Exercise or **K 41:** Drawing the Leg up in a Standing Position

5. **K 42:** Side Position Leg Lift or **K 43:** Standing Leg Lift

6. **K 45:** Heel Lift with One Leg or **K 44:** Heel Lift with Both Legs

7. **K 25:** Side Crunch or **K 27:** Beetle

8. **K 16:** Raising the Body from a Prone Position or **K 17:** Back Stretch from a Prone Position

Cool-down exercises and stretching

Two to three sets   8–12 or 15–20 repetitions per set (depending on the training target)

Static exercise K 16: 30–60 seconds per set

✖ K 31, K 32, K 37, K 40, K 42, K 45, K 25, K 16

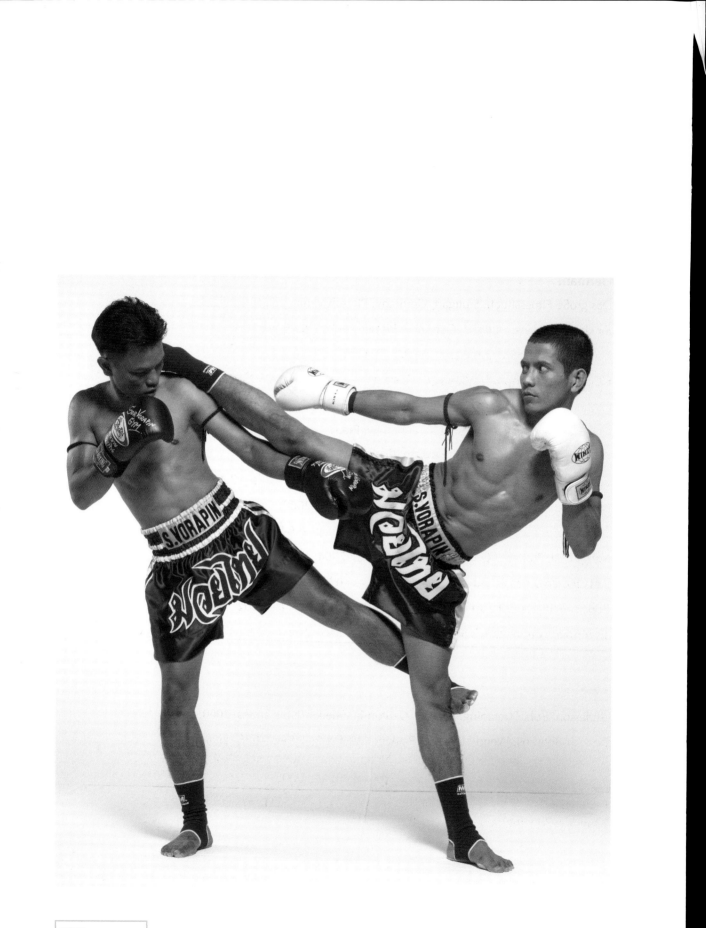

Other Books by Christoph Delp

English:

Muay Thai Basics: Introductory Thai Boxing Techniques. Berkeley, CA: Blue Snake Books, 2006.

Muay Thai: Advanced Thai Kickboxing Techniques. Berkeley, CA: Frog Ltd., 2004.

German:

Das große Fitnessbuch. Stuttgart, Germany: Pietsch Verlag, 2006.

Kickboxen basics. Stuttgart, Germany: Pietsch Verlag, 2006.

Best Stretching. Stuttgart, Germany: Pietsch Verlag, 2005.

Fitness für Kampfsportler. Stuttgart, Germany: Pietsch Verlag, 2005.

Fitness für Männer. Stuttgart, Germany: Pietsch Verlag, 2005.

Perfektes Hanteltraining. Stuttgart, Germany: Pietsch Verlag, 2005.

Thaiboxen basics. Stuttgart, Germany: Pietsch Verlag, 2005.

Bodytraining im Fitness-Studio. Stuttgart, Germany: Pietsch Verlag, 2004.

Fit für den Strand. Stuttgart, Germany: Pietsch Verlag, 2004.

Fitness für Frauen. Stuttgart, Germany: Pietsch Verlag, 2004.

Muay Thai. Stuttgart, Germany: Pietsch Verlag, 2004.

So kämpfen die Stars. Stuttgart, Germany: Pietsch Verlag, 2003.

Bodytraining für Zuhause. Stuttgart, Germany: Pietsch Verlag, 2002.

Thai-Boxen professional. Stuttgart, Germany: Pietsch Verlag, 2002.

Bibliography

Anderson, Bob. Stretching. Bolinas, California: Shelter Publications, 2000.

Boeckh-Behrens, Wend-Uwe and Buskies, Wolfgang. Fitness-Krafttraining. Die besten Übungen und Methoden für Sport und Gesundheit. 3. Auflage. Reinbeck bei Hamburg, Germany: Rowohlt Verlag, 2001.

Burger, Doris. Effektiv zum schlanken Bauch. Reinbeck bei Hamburg, Germany: Rowohlt Verlag, 2003.

Feil, Wolfgang and Wessinghage, Thomas. Ernährung und Training fürs Leben—20 Bausteine für Ihre Fitness. 2. Auflage. Nürnberg, Germany: Wessp Verlag, 2000.

Gießing, Jürgen. Ein-Satz-Training. Ein wissenschaftliches Konzept für schnellstmöglichen Muskelaufbau im Bodybuilding. Arnsberg, Germany: Novagenics Verlag, 2004.

Petersen, Ole. So einfach ist Fitness. Reinbeck bei Hamburg, Germany: Rowohlt Verlag, 2001.

Steffens, Thomas and Grüning, Martin. Das Laufbuch. Training, Technik, Ausrüstung. 7. Auflage. Reinbeck bei Hamburg, Germany: Rowohlt Verlag, 2003.

Steffny, Herbert and Pramann, Ulrich. Perfektes Lauftraining. München, Germany: Südwest, 2003.

Book Team

Performers

Steffen Bernhardt

Freestyle Karate (artistic karate)
Repeat Worldcup and
German Freestyle Karate Champion
www.g-ways.com

Christian Brell

Freestyle Karate (artistic karate)
World Freestyle Karate Champion (2001),
    Repeat European and German Freestyle
    Karate Champion
www.g-ways.com

Vanessa Florian

Kick-Boxing and Taekwondo
Repeat German Kick-Boxing Champion

Ernst G.

Model and martial arts athlete
(various disciplines)

Giovanni Nurchi

Kick-boxing

Repeat German and International Kick-Boxing
    Champion

Tui Sang

Model and martial arts athlete

(various disciplines)

Author

Christoph Delp

Diplom-Betriebswirt (master of business
    administration) and author

Fitness and Muay Thai (Thai-Boxing) trainer

Muay Thai trainer education in Thailand

from 1995 to 2001 with fight experience

Some publications: *Muay Thai Basics, Muay
    Thai: Advanced Thai Kickboxing Techniques*
    (2006), *Kickboxen basics* (2006), *Das große
    Fitnessbuch* (2006), *Fitness für Kampfsportler*
    (2005), *Thaiboxen basics* (2005).

www.christophdelp.com, www.muaythai.de

Also pictured:
Chawan Dasri (Thai-Boxing Champion)
Claudia Hein (Miss Germany 2004)
Janine Steiner (Kick-Boxing)
Jürgen Florian (German Kick-Boxing Champion)
Martin Albers (World and European Kick-Boxing Champion)
Natalia Hein (European Kick-Boxing Champion)
Nico Rings (Kick-Boxing)
Patiphan Simalai (Thai-Boxing Champion)
Somchok Homkaew (Thai-Boxing Champion)

Photographers

Nopphadol Viwatkamolwat www.astudioonline.com

Erwin Wenzel

Photo Acknowledgments

Photos by Nopphadol Viwatkamolwat: pp. v, 7, 10, 15, 34, 38, 51 (b), 53, 57, 72, 93, 95, 110, 123, 128 (a+b), 134, 135, 136, 138 (a+b), 139 (a+b), 143, 144 (a+b), 147, 149, 150, 151, 153 (a+b), 156, 157, 158, 159, 160, 161, 166, 167, 168, 169, 175, 177, 179, 180, 183, 184, 188, 190, 198, 199, 206, 207, 232, 233, 234, 235, 236, 237, 238, 242 (b+c).

All other photos by Erwin Wenzel.

Muay Thai Basics: Introductory Thaiboxing Techniques

Muay Thai, also referred to as Thai boxing, combines fitness training, self-defense, and competitive sport. In this hands-on guide, renowned trainer Christoph Delp presents the sport's history, development, rules, and equipment.

In the techniques section, he first details basic skills such as the correct starting position and footwork. Next he offers a complete list of all the attacking techniques and a selection of effective defensive and counterattacking strategies. All techniques are presented step-by-step by Thai champions from the famous Sor. Vorapin gym in Bangkok, showing readers the fine details of each technique. The training section provides detailed information about the structure, content, and planning of training regimens; this includes historical training methods, a stretching program, and training schedules. Suitable as both a self-training guide and a supplement to club training, *Muay Thai Basics* offers authoritative instruction for Thai boxers and other martial arts enthusiasts.

Muay Thai Basics: Introductory Thai Boxing Techniques

ISBN 1-58394-140-1

$19.95

Frog, Ltd./Blue Snake Books. Berkeley, California.

www.northatlanticbooks.com.
www.bluesnakebooks.com

Muay Thai: Advanced Thai Kickboxing Techniques

During the last twenty years, Muay Thai, also known as Thai boxing, has become popular around the world. Practitioners enjoy this martial art for fitness training, competitive sport, and self-defense.

Christoph Delp has studied intensively at many gyms and training camps in Thailand. In *Muay Thai: Advanced Thai Kickboxing Techniques,* he shares his experience of the people, history, and traditions of this exciting part of the country's extraordinary cultural heritage. Color photographs of Thai boxers demonstrate the techniques athletes must learn to succeed in professional or amateur contests, including well-proven offensive tactics as well as ways to counter an opponent's attacks. Historical Muay Thai techniques are also examined, which can be used by an experienced fighter to achieve a surprise victory.

Muay Thai: Advanced Thai Kickboxing Techniques

ISBN 1-58394-101-0

$19.95

Frog, Ltd./Blue Snake Books.
Berkeley, California.

www.northatlanticbooks.com,
www.bluesnakebooks.com